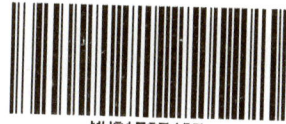

(S)HORT**ORDER**

MICROSOFT®
PhotoDraw 2000

MOLLY JOSS
JASON DUNN

Short Order Microsoft PhotoDraw 2000

International Standard Book Number: 0-7897-2048-5

Library of Congress Catalog Card Number: 9965643

Printed in the United States of America

First Printing: February 2000

02   01   00   4   3   2   1

Trademarks

Warning and Disclaimer

PUBLISHER
Greg Wiegand

ACQUISITIONS EDITOR
Karen Whitehouse

DEVELOPMENT EDITOR
Laura Norman

MANAGING EDITOR
Thomas Hayes

PROJECT EDITOR
Natalie Harris

COPY EDITOR
Cheri Clark

INDEXER
Chris Barrick

PROOFREADER
Maribeth Echard

TECHNICAL EDITOR
Jason Dunn

TEAM COORDINATOR
Lori Morgan

INTERIOR DESIGN
Karen Ruggles

COVER DESIGN
Aren Howell

LAYOUT TECHNICIANS
Cynthia Davis-Hubler
Brad Lenser

PRODUCTION
Dan Harris
George Poole

CONTENTS AT A GLANCE

TABLE OF CONTENTS

ABOUT THE AUTHOR

Molly Joss is an award-winning freelance writer and author who specializes in writing about the graphic arts and computer industries and who recently contributed the PhotoDraw chapters for Que's *Special Edition Using Office 2000* (Macmillan Publishing). She is a regular contributor to many desktop publishing and printing industry magazines; her articles have appeared in more than a dozen magazines and newsletters. Currently, she is a regular contributor to several magazines and writes a monthly computer software column for *Computer User*. Joss is also the author of several computer publishing books including *Clip Art Smart* (Rockport Publishers) and *Looking Good in Presentations* (Coriolis).

About the Coauthor

While earning a degree in Communications, **Jason Dunn** followed his entrepreneurial spirit by starting up his own company, Kensai Design & Communications. With a passion for consuming technology like it was water, Jason is a hybrid of next-generation business savvy and computer guru. As the President of Kensai Design & Communications (www.kensai.com), he lends his skills to a myriad of projects in the writing and graphical genre. He writes regularly for the Ulead WebUtilities site (www.webutilities.com) on everything from fonts to JavaScript rollovers. He's used every generation of Microsoft graphics programs, starting with Image Composer 1.0 up to the current topic of this book: PhotoDraw 2000.

DEDICATION

This book is dedicated to my grandfather, Fred Paniak, without whom I wouldn't be here at all. Blessings to you, dear grandfather—may peace find you wherever you are.

Jason Dunn

ACKNOWLEDGMENTS

No one writes a book alone, no matter whose name is on the cover. Because this book is part of a new series, many people were involved in the concept creation, visualization, and realization of this book. I want to thank all of the editors at Macmillan for allowing me to write this book, and for being so kind and helpful as we worked through the process. I could not have done it without them.

I also want to thank Waterside Productions for helping me find my way into the offices of Macmillan and for their help on the project. Good agents make good writers even better, I think.

Finally, I want to thank the PhotoDraw team at Microsoft for creating such a powerful new program. It has been my pleasure to write about PhotoDraw, and I hope you will enjoy the book and find it helpful.

Molly Joss

Thank you to Beth Millett for bringing me in on the first of many great projects, and to Laura Norman for being such a fantastic editor to work with. Laura, your wisdom, humor, and skill helped make this book a success!

Kudos to Microsoft for making software that continues to get better and better—I can't wait to see what's next!

For being my wonderful, graphical guinea pigs, thank you to Ashley S. and Ashley T., Christine, Cariann, Fred, Hejdi, Jacqueline, Mackenzie, Sarah, Valerie, and Vanessa. A big thank you to all my friends and family for your continued support, and a special thank you to Angela: Your support and encouragement were like oxygen to me during the intense writing and editing periods. Most importantly, thank you to the Creator who gave me talent and the willpower to strive for great things. *VIRTUTIS GLORIA MERCES.*

Jason Dunn

TELL US WHAT YOU THINK!

As the reader of this book, *you* are our most important critic and commentator. We value your opinion and want to know what we're doing right, what we could do better, what areas you'd like to see us publish in, and any other words of wisdom you're willing to pass our way.

As a publisher for Hayden MCP, I welcome your comments. You can fax, email, or write me directly to let me know what you did or didn't like about this book—as well as what we can do to make our books stronger.

Please note that I cannot help you with technical problems related to the topic of this book, and that due to the high volume of mail I receive, I might not be able to reply to every message.

When you write, please be sure to include this book's title and author as well as your name and phone or fax number. I will carefully review your comments and share them with the author and editors who worked on the book.

Greg Wiegand

Fax: 317-581-4666

Email: Hayden@mcp.com

Mail: Publisher
         Hayden MCP
         201 West 103rd Street
         Indianapolis, IN 46290 USA

INTRODUCTION

WELCOME TO SHORT ORDER PHOTODRAW 2000

Welcome to Short Order PhotoDraw 2000, your guide to PhotoDraw 2000, Microsoft's new image-editing program. Like the program itself, this book is designed to help you make the most of your image-editing time.

Our approach is to give you streamlined procedures—many of which are unique to this book—for using the software tools available in PhotoDraw 2000. Plus, we've included lots of tips and tricks aimed at helping you become a better designer—whether you're a professional or a part-time business user.

What Is PhotoDraw 2000?

PhotoDraw is a comprehensive suite of image-editing tools that includes literally thousands of easy-to-apply special effects. These special effects are effective and useful without modification but are also are easily changed to create an entirely new effect. The result is that with PhotoDraw you can do in several seconds what might take minutes or hours in other image-editing programs.

Unlike other image-editing programs that are geared toward creating images and performing minute edits, PhotoDraw gives you the power to quickly transform the look of any image, whether it's a text object, a photograph, or a piece of clip art.

PhotoDraw is one of the easiest image-editing programs to use and, with the array of special effects built into the program, one of the most versatile. Here are some of the things you can do with PhotoDraw:

- Customize images with special effects and editing tools

- Draw objects and enhance images with drawn objects

- Correct flaws in photographs

- Cut and crop photographs and other images

- Create professional-looking Web graphics

- Create unique text objects

- Manage your digital assets

PhotoDraw Highlights

A complete listing of PhotoDraw's capabilities would fill an entire book. But here are just a few of the highlights of the program that you will discover when you read this book:

- The inventory of special effects includes hundreds of ways to quickly change the appearance of any image, including clip art and photographs. For example, you can fill objects with solid colors, gradients, and even photographic images.

- In addition to the hundreds of ready-to-apply special effects that come with PhotoDraw, you also get thousands of clip art images, photographs, frames, templates, brushes, and line types. If you apply what you learn in this book to these images, you might find that you have so much image variety that you won't have to buy another piece of clip art or stock photography again!

- To help you make the most of digital-camera and other photographs you take yourself, Microsoft has built into PhotoDraw many photographic-related functions. With these functions, you can improve almost any photograph, including one with red-eye or one that is too light or too dark. You can even remove scratches from scanned photographic images.

How to Use This Book

This book is organized so that you can quickly find out how to use the various functions and capabilities in PhotoDraw. You are taken step-by-step through the functions, and in some chapters, you see step-by-step examples of how to use the software to achieve a certain effect.

To learn about creating and editing text, turn to Chapter 2 first to learn the basics. Then, move on to Chapter 3 to learn how to apply special effects, including gradients and other interesting fills, to text objects. To learn about creating 3-D text and adding shadows, check out the material in Chapters 10 and 11 that relates to text objects.

If you're interested in working with images first, start with Chapter 1 to learn the fundamentals of working with objects in PhotoDraw, and later move on to Chapters 8 and 11 to learn more about the special effects at your fingertips in PhotoDraw.

To learn how to create shapes and change their appearance, start with Chapters 6 and 7. Add to your knowledge by moving through Chapters 8 through 12. After you finish reading those chapters, you'll know all there is to know about drawing, painting, and editing images in PhotoDraw.

If you need help editing photographs, Chapter 4 has the most information about this topic. You'll also find interesting material related to working with photos in Chapters 6 and 8. In these two chapters, you'll learn how to select and apply special effects to photographs to accomplish the most in the least amount of time.

To learn how to use the many design templates included in PhotoDraw, check out Chapter 5. Not only will you learn about the kinds of templates available, but you will learn how to use them and even how to modify them to create new designs.

Web graphics are simple to create with PhotoDraw, and the material in Chapter 13 is where you should start.

The material in Chapter 8 about Designer Effects and Chapter 10 about creating 3-D images will also be helpful when you're creating unique Web graphic designs. Finally, check out the examples in Chapter 5 to learn how to make the most of the Web-graphics templates included in PhotoDraw.

To learn about saving your images into the Clip Gallery—PhotoDraw's digital asset manager—and how to use the Clip Gallery to organize your work, turn to Chapter 14. When you're ready to print your work, you'll find all the information and helpful hints you need in Chapter 15.

Finally, Chapter 16 provides you with information on the new Web Graphics features found only in the latest 2.0 release of PhotoDraw 2000.

CHAPTER 1

In this chapter you will learn how to...

Create a Cutout from a Predefined Shape

Use Edge Finder to Create a Cutout

Use Color to Create a Cutout

Duplicate Objects

Arrange Objects

Rotate and Flip Objects

Resize Objects

Align Objects

Layer Objects

Group and Ungroup Objects

PhotoDraw provides you with various ways to stretch your stock of clip art and other images, giving you all-new design possibilities. You can copy only part of an image by creating a cutout, resulting in a totally new object without ever changing the original. You can also create a new object by cutting away parts of another object or by duplicating the object and making some simple changes to the appearance of the duplicate object.

COMPOSING IMAGES FROM OBJECTS

Although the idea of creating new images might sound complicated, by using just a few simple steps you can change the look of an entire object by resizing, rotating, or flipping it. After you've used a few of these procedures to enhance your collection of objects, you can move on to composing pictures by arranging, aligning, and layering objects.

When you have every part of the image sized and arranged perfectly, you can ensure that things stay that way by grouping the objects.

All the tasks covered in this chapter can be used on image objects as well as on text objects, giving you additional (and reusable) materials for your designs with just a little extra time and effort.

Creating a Cutout from a Predefined Shape

The term "cutout" might make you think of taking a pair of scissors and cutting away portions of a picture you don't need. In PhotoDraw, though, creating a cutout doesn't require you to throw anything away. The software simply makes a copy of the area you've selected while leaving the original image intact.

1. Select the object or image you want to copy a portion from by clicking on it or opening the file.

2. Select Tools→Cut Out, and the Cut Out workpane with the gallery of the cutout shapes appears **(1.1)**.

3. Select By Shape from the list of options, and click on the shape you want the cutout to be. The image appears grayed out.

4. Click on the image and the cutout shape appears. Move the shape until it completely covers the area you want to cut out **(1.2)**.

Scroll down through the gallery of shapes, and you'll see dozens of shapes you can use besides the basic geometric ones shown here.

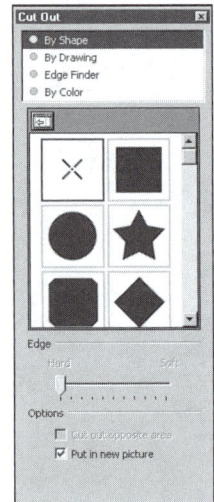

1.1

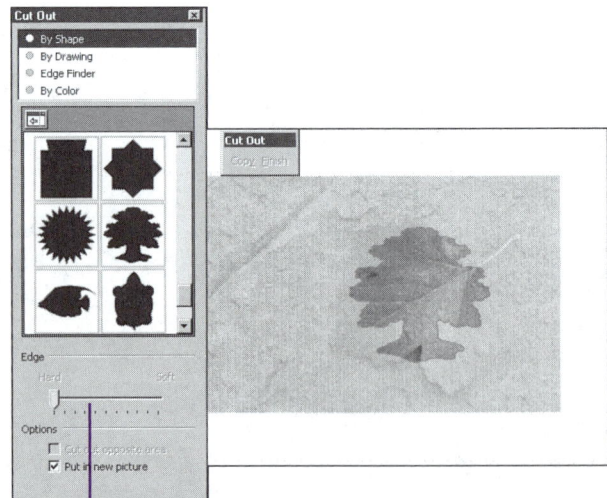

1.2 **If you want the edges of the copied area to look clean and crisp, leave the Edge slider set on Hard. If you want them to look a little fuzzy, slide the slider to the right toward the Soft setting.**

(N) O T E

To have PhotoDraw make the cutout as directed and leave it in the same image, dese-lect the Put in New Picture option on the Cut Out window.

5. When you have finished making your selections, click on the Cut Out Finish button. PhotoDraw makes the copy and, depending on the option you chose, shows the copy in the same window as the original or opens a new window and places the copy there **(1.3)**.

1.3   **You can resize the shape by clicking on one of the corners or sides and dragging the shape until it is the size you want.**

(T) I P

If you're going to blend your cutout with another picture, check to see how sharp or fuzzy the other picture is, and then match the edges of the cutout to the level of sharpness in the other image. That way, the cutout will blend in better.

(N) O T E

You can cut out a portion of an image using a shape by selecting Tools→Crop by Shape. You get to use the same predefined shapes as you do in this kind of cutout. However, when you crop an image, PhotoDraw makes the change to the original file rather than leaving the original file intact.

Using Edge Finder to Create a Cutout

With PhotoDraw, you are not restricted to using only predefined shapes for cutouts. If you want to cut an irregularly shaped area out of an image, use the Edge Finder to select the portion of the image you want to copy. With it, you can control the selection area more precisely than with any other cutout method.

1. Open a file and select the image you want to cutout a portion of; select Tools→Cut Out. The Cut Out workpane appears.

2. Select Edge Finder from the list of options in the workpane, and the Edge Finder controls appear (1.4).

3. Set the width of the Edge Finder either by typing a number or by adjusting the number using the slider. The higher the number, the more area PhotoDraw will search in order to find the edge of the object.

4. Begin to draw a line around the outline of the image area you want to copy by clicking on a point in the image. To get the cleanest outline possible, zoom in on the image before making your selections. This method takes longer but ensures a clean object cut. Continue to draw a line around the area by clicking when you come to a curve or turn.

1.4

You can control the degree of hardness the edge of the cutout will have by adjusting the settings on the Path Smoothness slider on the Cut Out workpane after you create the outline but before you click on the Cut Out button.

Take your time drawing the outline, and click frequently to make many small segments. You will have to start over and create a new outline if you don't like the results of the Edge Finder. Click the Reset button to start the process again.

1.5

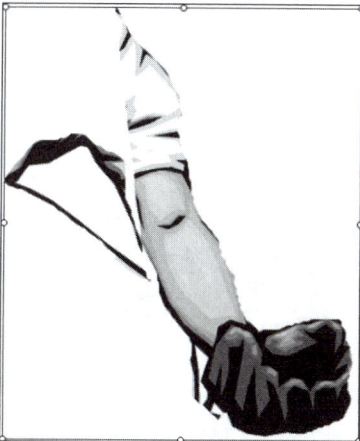

1.6

5. Double-click to stop the outlining process. PhotoDraw shows a dotted line around the area you have outlined. The rest of the image not selected by the outline area is grayed out (1.5).

6. Click the Edge Finder button on the floating Cut Out toolbar, and PhotoDraw makes a copy of the image area within the dotted outline. The cutout appears in a new window and the original image is left intact (1.6).

(N) O T E

For more flexibility, you can use the By Drawing option on the Cut Out list in the workpane to select an area to copy, and it works in much the same way as the Edge Finder. However, the Edge Finder is much easier to use and just as accurate—most of the time.

(N) O T E

To copy the portion of a picture outside the selection area, outline the area you don't want to copy, and then select the Cut Out Opposite Area option in the Cut Out workpane.

Using Color to Create a Cutout

Using color as a means of telling PhotoDraw what areas to copy is a good way to copy areas of an image that are of different colors than the rest of the image. It's also an efficient way to copy irregular snippets of an image (1.7). Clicking on areas that are the same color tells PhotoDraw you want to make a cutout using those areas.

Using the Cut Out tool that lets you cut out shapes by color is a good way to cut out colored images with irregular shapes such as this image has.

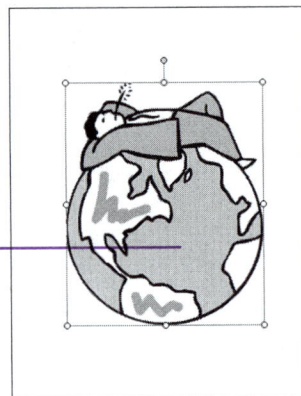

1.7

1. Select the image you want to create a color cutout from, and select Tools→Cut Out. The Cut Out workpane appears.

2. Select By Color from the list of options in the workpane, and the By Color controls appear in the Cut Out workpane.

3. Select the portion of the image you want to copy by clicking on the color. PhotoDraw turns the area another color (the default is light purple) to show that it has been selected (1.8).

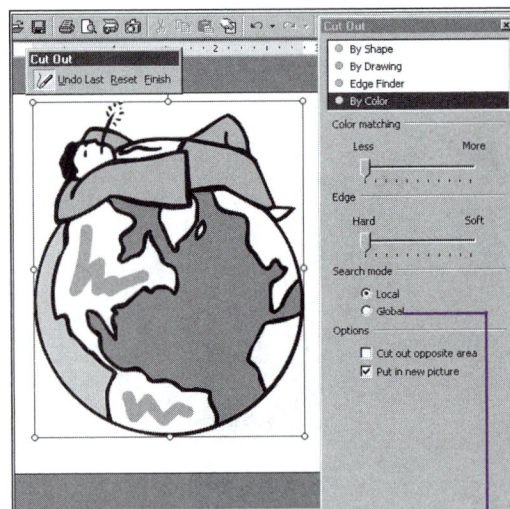

1.8

The Global setting allows you to select all areas of a single color at one time.

(N) O T E

Use the Color Matching slider to tell PhotoDraw approximately how many shades of the selected color you want included in the copy. If there are many shades of the same color, set the slider more to the right; to select only one or two, set it more to the left.

1.9

4. Continue clicking on colored areas to select them. Each color turns into a different color to show that that area has been selected. When you have finished making your selections, click on the Finish button on the floating Cut Out toolbar.

5. If the option Put in New Picture is selected, PhotoDraw opens another window and shows the area that has been cut out using this method (1.9); otherwise, the cutout will appear in the original file along with the original, intact image.

T I P

Global is a good Search Mode setting to use if there are more than one or two areas of the same color you want to copy. Use Local to restrict the areas to only those colors around where you have clicked.

T I P

If you don't want the area that is being copied to look blurred or fuzzy, keep the Edge slider set to Hard to get a clean, crisp edge on the area that is copied.

Duplicating Objects

If you want to use more than one
copy of an object in your design,
you can place the object in your new
image multiple times, or you can
duplicate it after you have placed
one copy in your design. Because
duplicating objects is a one-step procedure and copying and pasting
requires two steps, duplicating is
more efficient.

1. To use the Picture List method,
   open the picture list by selecting View→Picture List. The
   Picture List panel opens on the
   left side of the window (1.10).

2. Scroll through the picture list
   to find the image or object you
   want to bring into your in-
   progress design.

3. Click on the image or object
   and drag it into the active
   work area. PhotoDraw duplicates the image and places the
   duplicate in the active work
   area (1.11).

**You can move the
picture list around
the work area by
clicking on it and
dragging it to the
new position.**

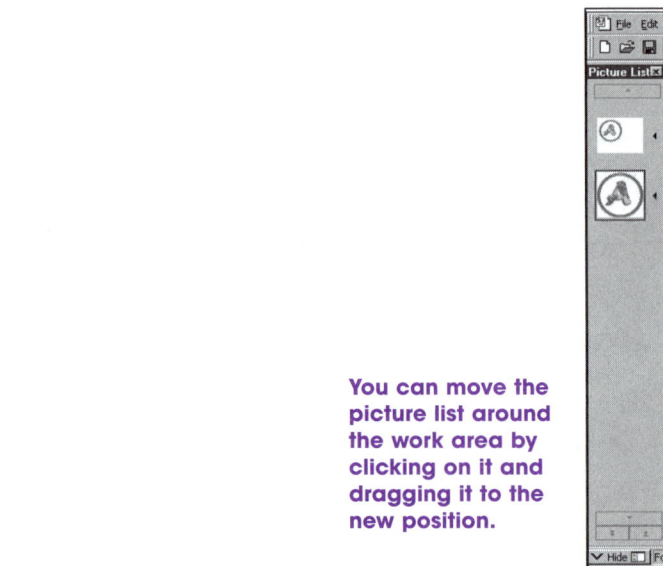

1.10

1.11

(T) I P

*Try this neat special effect: Duplicate an
object and then change the appearance of the
copy by changing the fill or the color. Place
the edited copy behind and slightly to the left
or right of the original to create a shadow
effect.*

Arranging Objects

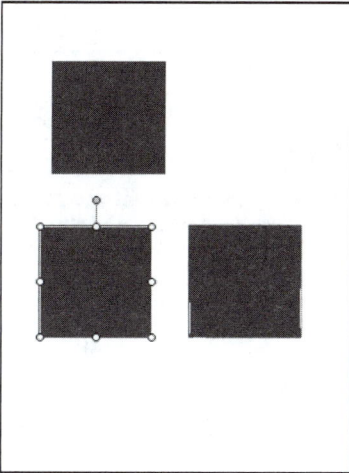

1.12

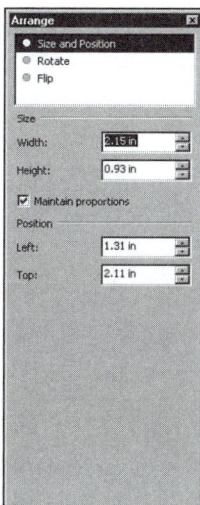

1.13

When you're arranging your objects, PhotoDraw enables you to use the coordinates in the status bar to help line things up by eye, or to be even more precise, you can type the exact coordinates. Another way to arrange objects is by aligning them using the procedures described in tasks later in this chapter.

1. Click on one of the items in your document and, while holding down the mouse button, drag the object to move it to its new position.

2. Repeat with each object in the design until you have placed each in the desired position **(1.12)**.

3. To be absolutely precise about where you place an object, click on the object and then select Arrange→Arrange. The Arrange workpane opens**(1.13)**.

continues

(T) I P

If you are working with an existing design, begin by checking to be sure that the items are not grouped together. If they are, turning off the grouping will make it possible to arrange the items differently. All objects to be arranged must be in the same document.

Arranging Objects continued

4. Enter the distance you want the top of the object area to be from the top of the picture area by entering a number in the Top box **(1.14)**.

5. Enter the distance you want the left side of the object area to be from the left side of the picture area by entering a number in the Left box. Select another object and repeat the preceding steps until all objects are arranged as desired.

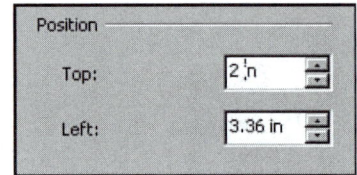

Position	
Top:	2 in
Left:	3.36 in

1.14 **To move an image to the upper-left side of the image area, enter 0 (zero) in both the Top and the Left boxes.**

(N) O T E

PhotoDraw also enables you to make duplicates of an image or object and precisely arrange these copies on a single sheet of paper. You do this by printing reprints of the image (see Chapter 15 for more information).

(T) I P

It's a good idea to group images (Arrange→Group) after you have them lined up the way you want them to be. Doing so avoids the possibility of accidentally moving one out of alignment later.

Rotating and Flipping Objects

1.15

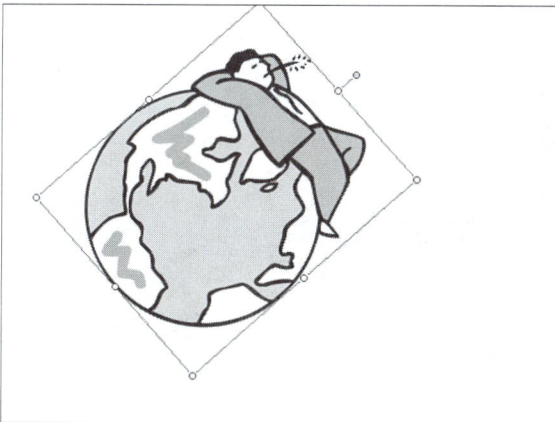

1.16

Rotating and flipping objects are simple changes you can make in one or two steps. Even though they are easy to do, they are still powerful ways to change the appearance of an object. Use one procedure to change the appearance slightly; combine these two procedures with resizing (covered later in this chapter) to make more radical changes.

1. Select the object you want to rotate by clicking on it. The image is outlined in a rectangle, and a rotation handle with a green dot at the end appears at the top of the image rectangle **(1.15)**.

2. Click on the green dot and rotate the image while holding down the mouse button. Release the mouse button when you are satisfied with the rotation of the object **(1.16)**.

3. If you want to rotate the object to the left or right, select Arrange→Rotate and then Rotate Left or Rotate Right.

continues

(T) I P

If you know what angle of rotation you want to use, type the number using the Custom Rotate feature. You'll save time and have precise control over the rotation that way.

Rotating and Flipping Objects continued

4. To rotate the object a precise number of degrees, select Arrange→Rotate→Custom Rotate. The Arrange workpane opens and Rotate is highlighted. To select a rotation of 0°, 90°, 180°, or 270° from the gallery of rotation settings, click on the appropriate icon **(1.17)**.

5. To flip an object, select the object you want to flip, and choose Arrange→Flip. The pop-up menu of flip options (Flip Horizontal, Flip Vertical, and Flip Both) appears **(1.18)**.

6. Select the kind of flip you want and PhotoDraw flips the object.

To specify a degree of rotation other than these, type a number in the Custom box. You can enter a figure between –360° and 360° in fractions of a degree. If you get confused, set the rotation to 0° and start over.

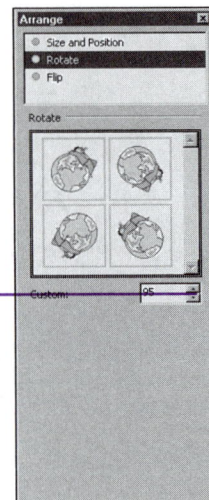

1.17

(T) I P

To make a pair of objects, take one object, duplicate it, and flip the duplicate in the opposite direction from the original. Place the two side by side like bookends.

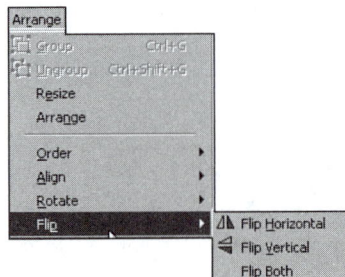

1.18

(N) O T E

Another way to flip an object is to do it through the Arrange workpane. Select Arrange→Arrange and the Arrange workpane appears. Select Flip from the list of options in the workpane, and icons of the four flip options appear (No Flip, Flip Horizontal, Flip Vertical, and Flip Horizontal and Vertical) **(1.19)**. *Click on the icon of the flip you want, and PhotoDraw applies the flip.*

Use the No Flip option to undo a flip you make using one of the other three flip options.

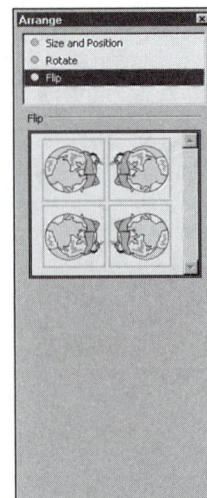

1.19

Resizing Objects

1.20

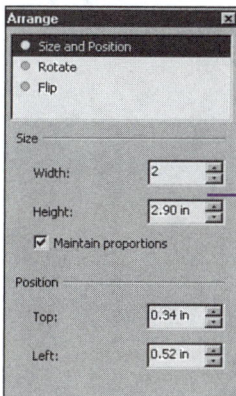

1.21

The current dimensions of the selected object automatically appear in the Width and Height boxes.

If you want to change the proportions of an object as well as one dimension, turn off the Maintain Proportions box and change either the Height or the Width value.

Rarely are images the exact size you'd like them to be, particularly when you are combining images to create a composite design. You can change the size of any object by clicking and dragging to enlarge or reduce it.

1. Click on the object you want to resize to select it. A rectangle with the rotation handle at the top appears around the object and small circles appear on the outline of the object.

2. To resize the object while keeping the proportions the same, click on one of the corner circles and drag that side of the image outward to make the image larger or move it inward to make the object smaller (1.20).

3. To make the object wider or narrower, click on one of the circles on the sides and drag in or out. To make the object taller or shorter, click on one of the circles at the top or bottom of the object, and drag up or down.

(N) O T E

To resize an object more precisely, select Arrange→Arrange, and select Size and Position from the list in the workpane. Enter the new dimensions of the object into the width and height boxes. PhotoDraw resizes the object (1.21).

Aligning Objects

You can arrange objects by using their coordinates or by eye, but it's much easier to align objects by using the align functions in PhotoDraw. PhotoDraw aligns objects along their sides or centers, just as you would do manually—but this method is a lot more precise than doing it by eye, which makes it the fastest and most effective way to line up objects along invisible horizontal or vertical lines.

1. Select all the objects you want to align by holding down the Shift key while clicking on the objects (1.22).

2. Select Arrange→Align, and the pop-up menu of alignment choices appears.

3. To align the objects along the left side (1.23) (the left side of the image area, not the borders of the images themselves), select Align Left from the pop-up menu.

4. To align the objects along the right side (the right side of the image area, not the borders of the images themselves), select Align Right from the pop-up menu.

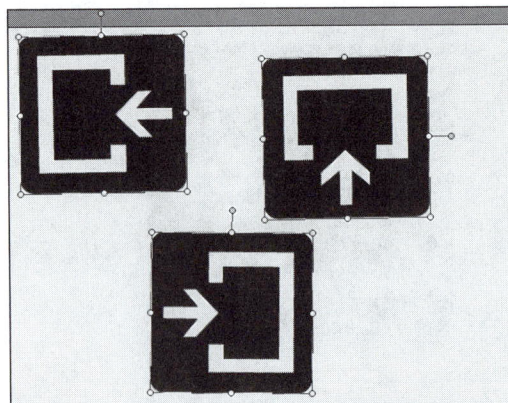

1.22   **The only way to keep objects from overlapping when they are aligned is to move the objects away from one another first.**

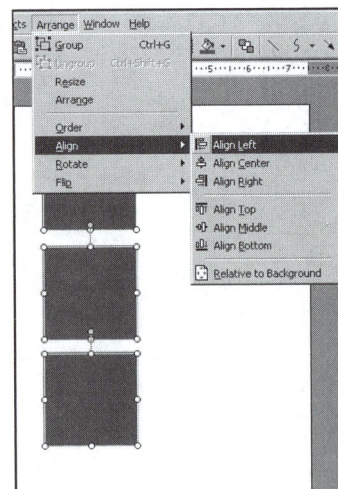

1.23

(N) O T E

The pop-up menu of alignment choices has three sections. All alignment selections can be made relative to the objects themselves or to the entire picture area.

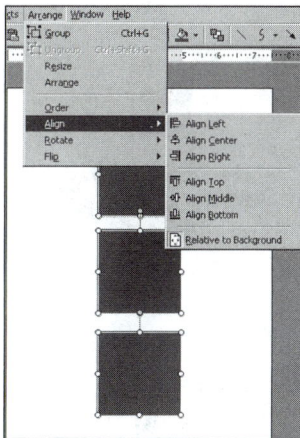

1.24

1.25

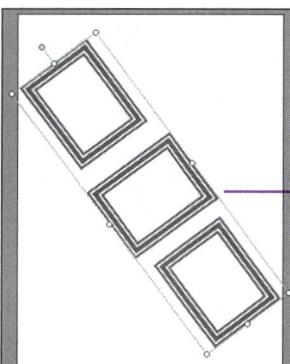

These objects were first aligned along their centers and then grouped (Arrange→Group). The group was then rotated as shown.

1.26

5. To make the objects align across the vertical middle of their images areas **(1.24)**, select Align Center from the pop-up menu.

6. To make the objects align along their top, select Align Top from the pop-up menu.

7. To make the objects align along their bottom sides, select Align Bottom from the pop-up menu.

8. To make the objects align along their horizontal middles, select Align Middle from the pop-up menu **(1.25)**.

(T) I P

You can combine one kind of alignment from the first section on the pop-up menu with one kind of alignment from the second section. For example, you can make the objects align left and then along their bottoms, but not combine left alignment with right alignment.

(T) I P

*To align objects along an invisible diagonal line, first align the objects horizontally or vertically; then, group them and rotate the resulting object until you get the kind of line you want **(1.26)**.*

Layering Objects

Imagine piling your objects one on top of another to achieve a look of depth or to add a background to a design. You do this by layering or ordering objects, and it's a good way to add the look of depth to an image. It's also a good way to ensure that part of an object does not show or print over part of another object (unless that's your intention).

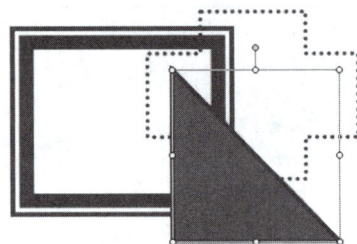

1.27

1. Select the object you want to be behind all the others. Choose Arrange→Order and the pop-up menu of layering options appears.

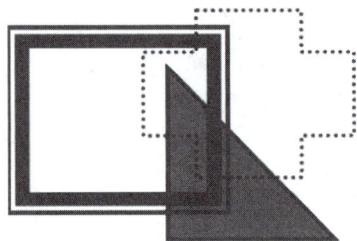

1.28

2. Click on Send to Back and PhotoDraw places that object in the very back of the picture area (1.27).

3. Click on the object you want to place in front of all the others, and select Bring to Front from the pop-up menu. PhotoDraw places that object on top of the others (1.28).

(T) I P

You can also order objects by starting at the back and working upward or by starting at the top and working downward. Any scheme will do, as long as you pick one and stick with it. Otherwise, you might get confused trying to decide which objects belong behind and in front.

Grouping and Ungrouping Objects

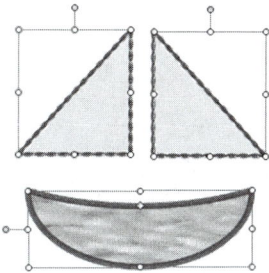

1.29

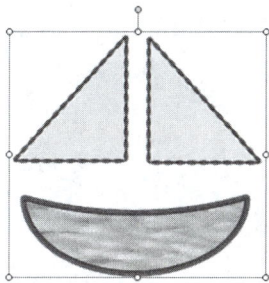

1.30

In this gallery of images, each image was grouped only with its frame, so that the framed images could be moved around easily to determine the best arrangement.

1.31

Selecting objects to stay together as if they were elements of a larger object is the only way to ensure that all the arranging and layering you've done will remain intact. You "glue" the objects together in their relative positions by grouping them. To edit or move the individual objects in a grouped object, you must first turn off the grouping (ungroup).

1. To group two or more objects, first arrange the objects as desired.

2. Select all the objects to be included in a single group by holding down the Shift key and clicking on each object **(1.29)**.

3. Select Arrange→Group and PhotoDraw makes one grouped object from the individual objects. A new image-area rectangle appears around the outside of the entire grouped object **(1.30)**.

4. To ungroup, select the grouped object and choose Arrange→ Ungroup. PhotoDraw turns off the grouping.

(T) I P

*Make one large group in a design if you are using only a few objects. If you are using more, consider making a few groups of a few objects each **(1.31)**. You'll spend less time later ungrouping and disturbing layers to reach an object you want to edit.*

CHAPTER 2

In this chapter you will learn how to...

Create and Edit Plain Text

Format Text

Create and Edit Designer Text

Underline a Text Object

Bend Text

Align and Group Text Objects

PhotoDraw gives you many ways to create plain or exotic text, with many more options for controlling the appearance of text than you can achieve in word processing or other image-editing programs. For example, you can change from plain to outline text with just a few steps. Or you can curve text along an arc or a circle.

CREATING AND EDITING TEXT OBJECTS

In a few steps, you can quickly create a piece of plain text and move on to other parts of an image. If you want to invest some more time, you can create wonderfully unique text objects that look more like art than text.

After you've learned even a few ways to change the appearance of a basic text object, you'll be able to think of creative ways to use text as images. For example, you know that text in a logo is never regular-looking text, so you'll be able to make your own logos after you learn how to get creative with text objects.

You can also create text objects that you can use as attention-getters on other printed pieces such as flyers and posters. You can also create special text elements to add additional interest to presentations and Web pages.

Start by learning the simpler text editing procedures outlined at the beginning of this chapter and then move on to the more complex procedures near the end. Along the way, don't be afraid to take some time out to practice with the special effects you see on the workpanes. In a short time, you'll see how powerful and how easy the text-editing features in PhotoDraw are.

Creating and Editing Plain Text

In PhotoDraw, you create and edit plain text by using a workpane box where you enter and edit text. Changes made to the text in the workpane are immediately visible in the open document onscreen. You can create text in PhotoDraw or copy and paste text from another program (such as Word). After you've added text to your page, you can manipulate it by using fills, outlines, transformation tools, or other object enhancements such as 3D or Designer Effects to create extraordinary logos or other text objects.

1. Select Insert→Text, and the Text workpane appears with the phrase "Your text here" highlighted (2.1).

2. Type your text into the workpane. As you type, the text appears on the document page inside a text box with a selection handle (2.2).

3. When you have finished typing your text, close the Text workpane to finish.

Group chunks of text together in one text block that will be formatted in the same way so that you can make formatting and appearance changes faster and more efficiently.

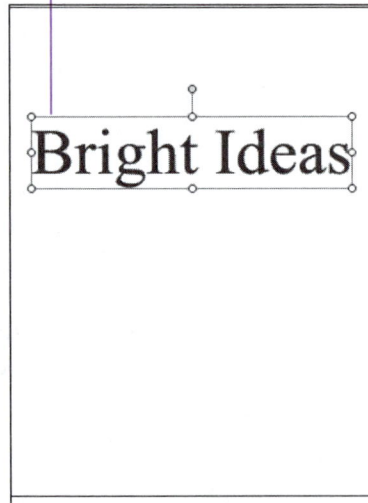

2.1

2.2

Ⓣ I P

To delete a text object from an image, click on the object to select it, and press the Delete key or choose Edit→Delete.

Bright Ideas

To enlarge the area you have for typing or pasting text, click on the icon right above the text window and the area will expand. Click on the icon again to return to the smaller text area.

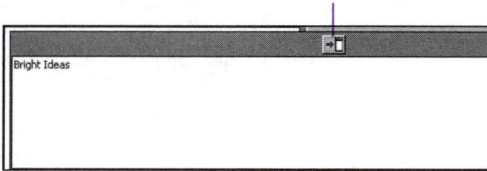

Bright Ideas

2.3

4. If you need to make changes to the text after closing the Text workpane, you must click on the text you want to edit and select Edit→Text or Format→Text to open a text workpane (2.3).

5. The Text workpane reopens, allowing you to edit your text. The text on the document page changes as you type. Close the Text Workpane to finish the editing process.

(T) I P

If you want to use text from another file or image, you can paste into a Text workpane the text you have copied onto the Clipboard. PhotoDraw replaces all the text attributes, such as font and size of font, with the current text selections in PhotoDraw.

(T) I P

There is no way to check your spelling in PhotoDraw, so you'll have to do it manually or spell-check text in a word processing program before you copy and paste it into a PhotoDraw image.

Formatting Text

After you've created text in PhotoDraw, you will want to take advantage of the various formatting options available on the Text workpane. You can apply many familiar text formats such as font, size, and color. You can also do more with text than you can in a word processor, such as applying artistic effects or making the object look three-dimensional.

1. Select the text you want to change the format settings for by double-clicking on it. Select Format→Text and the Text workpane appears with the text you want to edit in the workpane.

2. To change the font, click on the font drop-down list below the text area, and scroll up or down to find the font you want to use **(2.4)**. Select the font, and the selected text in the document changes automatically.

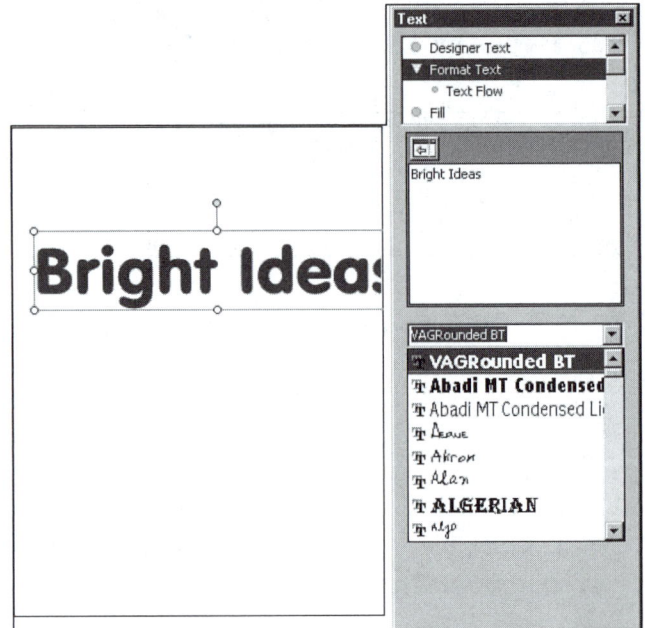

2.4

Ⓝ O T E

PhotoDraw "remembers" the font and other text attributes used for the last text object that was created, so anytime you create a new text object it is automatically formatted with those same attributes. PhotoDraw also applies those format settings to any text you import by using the Clipboard.

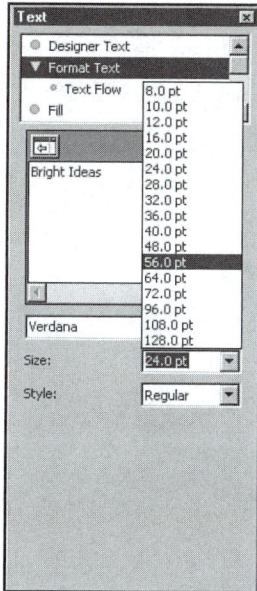

2.5

2.6

3. To change the size of the font, either select a size from the drop-down list of sizes beneath the text area in the Text work-pane or manually type the size you want into the Size box **(2.5)**.

4. To change the type style, choose a new style from the Style drop-down list. When you make your selection, the type-style change takes place automatically **(2.6)**.

continues

(T) I P

If you know which font, font size, and style you want to use for the text object, select those characteristics before you begin to type the text in the Text window.

(T) I P

All formatting changes are applied to all the words in a text group. To apply changes to a single word or letter only, make that word or letter a separate text object.

Formatting Text continued

5. To rotate the text object either horizontally or vertically, select the object by double-clicking it on the document page, and then select Text Flow from the list in the top of the Text workpane. The workpane changes to show two orientation options: horizontal and vertical. Select the option that suits your needs, and the text object on the page immediately changes position according to your selection **(2.7)**.

6. To change the alignment of text in a multiple-line text object, choose your desired alignment from the drop-down list in the Align area of the Text dialog box. The text alignment changes on the page depending on your selection **(2.8)**.

2.7

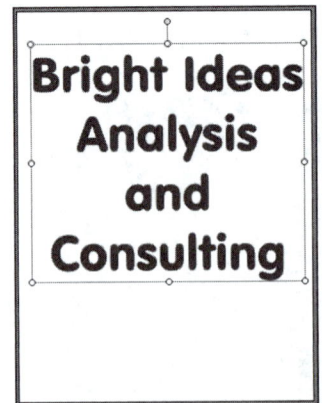

2.8

ⓉI P

If you are editing text or changing formats and find that you cannot make any changes or open the Text window, be sure that the Hide/Show icon in the lower-right side of the work area says Hide and not Show. If it says Show, click on the icon and the Text window will appear; you can then make your edits and changes.

Creating and Editing Designer Text

2.9

2.10

If you want to add flair to your text objects but don't want to take a lot of time making them look great, use the Designer Text feature in PhotoDraw. You can get spectacular results in a few minutes. You can also apply many of PhotoDraw's special effects to Designer Text for even more interesting results.

1. Select Insert→Text and the Text workpane appears.

2. Type the words you want to turn into Designer Text, and the text appears on the document page behind the Text window.

3. Select Designer Text from the list of options at the top of the Text window, and the Designer Text Gallery appears (2.9).

4. Double-click on the Designer Text "look" you want to apply to the text. PhotoDraw automatically applies the look to the text object (2.10).

continues

(T) I P

It's easy to try several different Designer Text looks within a few minutes by selecting Edit→Undo to revert to the look previously selected. Use Undo multiple times to get back to the original look of the text.

Creating and Editing Designer Text continued

5. To change the font, size, or style of the text without losing the Designer Text look, click on the Format Text item in the list of options, and the size and style controls appear in the Text workpane.

6. Customize your new Designer Text by making changes to any or all of the formatting options available (2.11).

Choose a new font, size, or style for your Designer Text by using these drop-down lists.

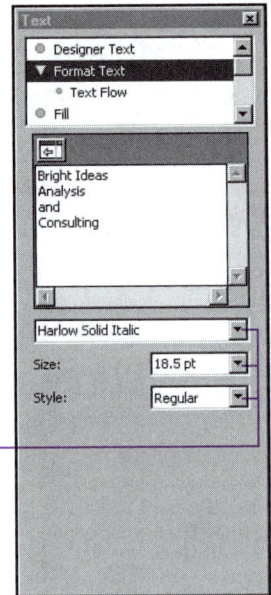

2.11

(N) O T E

After you have created a Designer Text object, you can make all the same text edits that you can to plain text, including rotating the object, changing colors in the object, and applying text and image special effects. With these features, you have the opportunity to create exciting, attention-getting text in only a few minutes.

(T) I P

Be sure to experiment with the style and font used in your type object after you have selected and applied a Designer Text style. With a few of these changes, you can create mix-and-match sets of text objects that share the same colors and basic style but look slightly different (2.12).

2.12

Underlining a Text Object

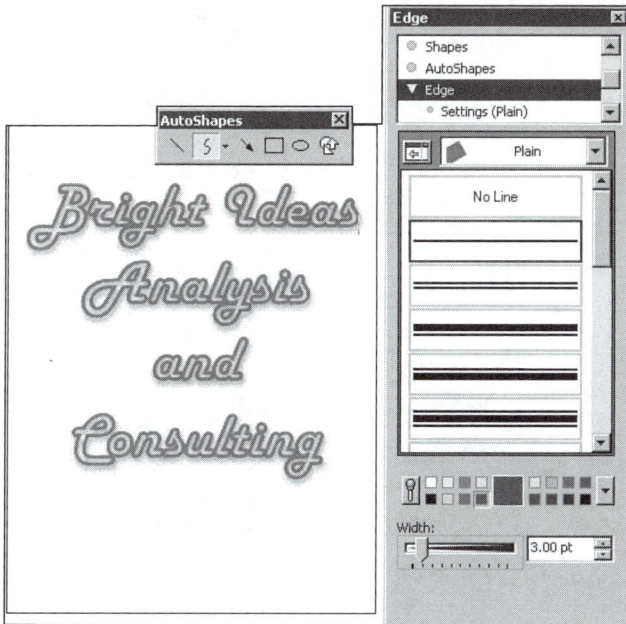

2.13

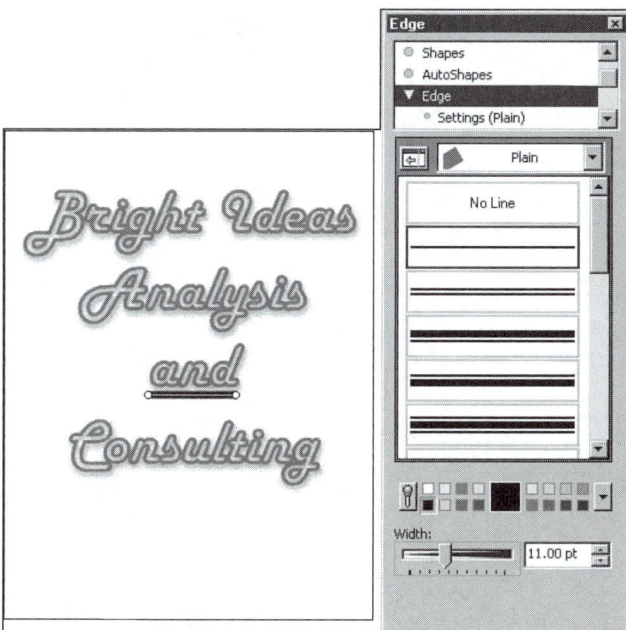

2.14

At times, you might want to underline a word, several words, or even a few lines of text. PhotoDraw has no automatic way of underlining text as you would in a word processing program. But there is a simple way to simulate the look of underlined text.

1. Create or select the word or text object you want to underline.

2. Select Tools→Draw Tools. The Edge workpane appears, showing the gallery of lines (2.13), and the cursor state changes into a cross shape.

3. To draw a straight line, select the straight line icon from the Autoshapes toolbar by clicking on the icon.

4. Draw a single straight line under the word or text object by clicking where you want the line to start.

5. Drag the cursor to draw the line; then double-click to stop drawing and end the line (2.14).

continues

(T) I P

Although underlines in plain text are normally thin, unbroken lines, you can use all the line styles to create underlines for more dramatic-looking text. Try using a double or dashed line to spice up the look.

Underlining a Text Object continued

6. To adjust the width of the line, use the up or down arrows or type a number in the Width box at the bottom of the window **(2.15)**.

7. To change the color of the line, click on the down arrow to open the color selection drop-down list, or use the Eyedropper tool to sample a color from another image **(2.16)**.

8. Move the line up or down to adjust the amount of space between the text object and the line.

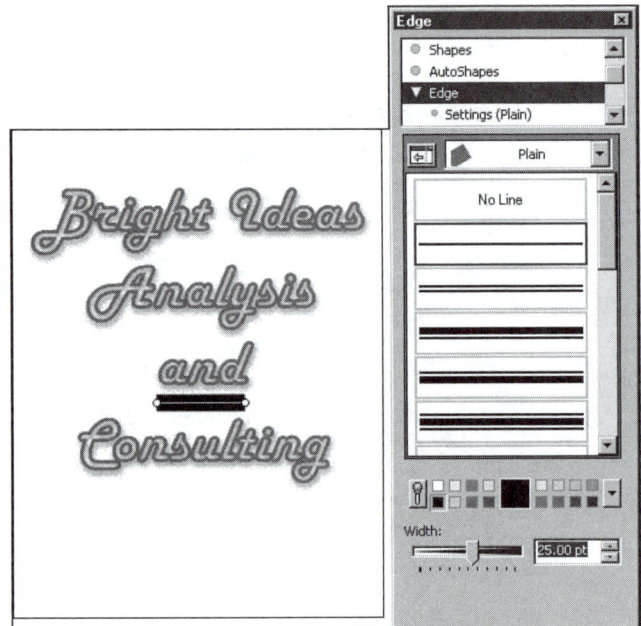

2.15

(T) I P

You can specify the line style and color before you draw the line rather than after, to save time. PhotoDraw will retain both the style and the color settings so that you can use them the next time you draw a line.

2.16

(N) O T E

Unless you change the placement of the line to put it behind the text object (Arrange→ Order→Send to Back), the line will cut through the descenders of your letters (the parts of the letters that hang below the bottoms of the rest of the letters). If the text and line are the same color, this change will not be necessary, but it's important to do it if your text is one color and the underline another.

Bending Text

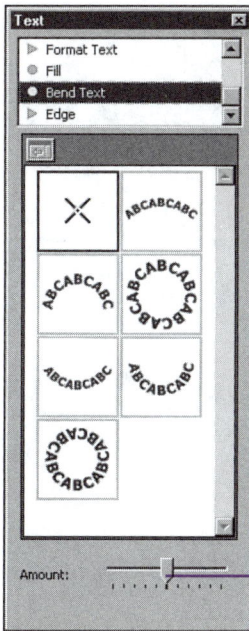

You can control the amount of the bend by sliding the Amount slider from left to right. Setting the pointer in the middle makes the line straight. Sliding it to the left bends the line upward; sliding it to the right bends the line downward.

2.17

2.18

Sometimes you might want to liven up your images by bending a line of text. For example, you might want to curve a line of text to fit around an image to create a logo. Or you might want to fit the text around a shape. You can create these special effects with just a few steps after you've selected the image you want to put text around.

1. In a new image window, insert the image you want to bend text around.

2. Create the text object (Insert→Text) and place it above or below the image.

3. Select Bend Text from the list in the Text workpane, and a gallery of examples for bending text appears. The options include quarter circles, half circles, and a full circle (2.17). Click on the curving option you want to use and the text object bends accordingly.

4. To check out the effect of various options, simply click on another option. PhotoDraw first straightens the text object and then applies the new curve.

continues

(T) I P

You can apply the bending effects to vertical lines of text, too. Try bending a vertical line of text to make it fit around the left or right side of an image (2.18).

Bending Text continued

5. Arrange the image and text so that you can size the text object properly, by clicking on the image and adjusting its size or location with the selection handles. Then put the image behind the text object by selecting Arrange→Order and selecting either Send to Back or Send Backward **(2.19)**.

6. If you need to resize the text object so that the text curves around the image, click on the text object and then click on one of the corner selection handles of the box that appears around the text. Drag the corner in or out to resize the text **(2.20)**.

7. Finish by grouping the text and the image together so that they can be moved around as one object.

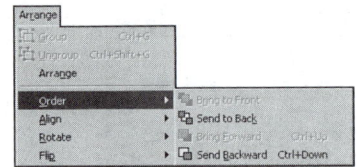

2.19

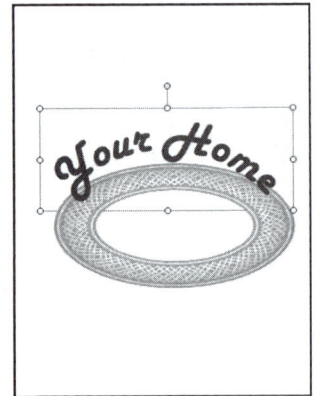

2.20

You can remove the bend from a text group by clicking on the × in the upper-left side of the gallery.

(N) O T E

Send to Back moves the selected object to the very back of the design so that it is behind every other object in the design. Send Backward moves the selected object only one level back, and other objects might still be layered behind it. Imagine the difference between being sent to the end of the line and being asked to stand behind the person behind you in line.

Aligning and Grouping Text Objects

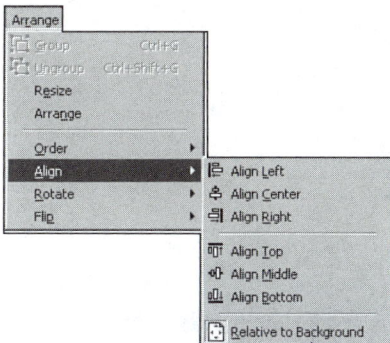

```
Arrange
  Group          Ctrl+G
  Ungroup   Ctrl+Shift+G
  Resize
  Arrange

  Order          ▶
  Align          ▶   ⌷ Align Left
  Rotate         ▶   ⌷ Align Center
  Flip           ▶   ⌷ Align Right

                     ⌷ Align Top
                     ⌷ Align Middle
                     ⌷ Align Bottom

                     ⌷ Relative to Background
```

2.21   PhotoDraw makes the alignments relative to the objects themselves and not the shape of the page unless you select Relative to Picture Area (the last item on the pop-up list) before you select the type of alignment.

Sometimes, you will want to arrange two or more text objects so that you can add some embellishment such as underlining or a box around objects. Aligning the objects and then grouping them is a good way to accomplish this task.

1. Select the objects you want to align by holding down the Shift key and then clicking on the desired objects.

2. Select Arrange→Align, and the pop-up list of alignment options appears (2.21).

3. Scroll down the list to select the alignment option you want to use.

4. If you want to combine alignment effects, select the first alignment (left, center, or right), and then while the objects are still selected, make the second alignment choice (top, middle, or bottom).

5. When you have finished making your alignment changes and while the objects are still selected, group them as one unit by selecting Arrange→Group.

(T) I P

Anytime you use two items as pairs, it's a good idea to align and group them, but if you use a text object between them, align the text object by eye to get the best results.

CHAPTER 3

In this chapter you will learn how to...

Change Text Outlines

Apply Text Fills

Change Texture Fills and Colors

Change Designer Gradient Fills and Colors

Apply Two-Color Gradient Fills and Colors

Change Picture Fills and Colors

Apply Artistic Fills to Text Objects

Combine Text Effects

Aside from the Designer Text effects covered in Chapter 2, PhotoDraw supplies various other special effects you can apply to text objects. These effects include special fills such as solid colors, textures, and gradients.

Using the same procedures of creating text, filling it and outlining it can give you endless options. For example, a simple special effect is to create a text object and then fill it with a color and outline it in another. If you're looking for a little more excitement in the image, fill the text object with a fabric texture and outline it in a color selected from the texture.

APPLYING SPECIAL EFFECTS TO TEXT OBJECTS

With these special effects, you can create outstanding text for use on Web sites, business stationery, and even posters. If you combine a special fill with some of the special effects such as outlines and bending, you can produce some spectacular-looking text objects in less than 30 minutes.

In this chapter, you will learn how to change the outlines of a text object, apply and change fills of all kinds, and combine text effects.

Changing Text Outlines (Edges)

You can change the appearance of a text object by changing the look of the edge of the text. Making it thicker makes the text look heavier, whereas making it thinner causes the text object to attract less attention. When designing text, keep in mind your intended use. Whether for a company logo or combined with other objects on a poster or other print or Web materials, the outline can help the text become the more dominant object, or when used subtly, it can allow the text to be part of an overall look. You'll find that a simple change in outline can make a drastic change in otherwise bland or overwhelming text.

1. Click on the text object to select it, and then select Format→Text to open the Text workpane. Select Edge from the list; a list of outline options appears (3.1).

2. Select the kind of outline you want to use from the pop-up list of the four brush options (Plain, Artistic, Theme, and Photo) (3.2), and a gallery of the brush outlines appears.

3.1

Here is a text object shown with four different edges: (1) a plain edge, (2) the charcoal artistic brush edge, (3) the brown rope photo edge, and (4) the Blends1 theme brush. All were done at 40-point widths. The original object without the edge is shown below the four examples.

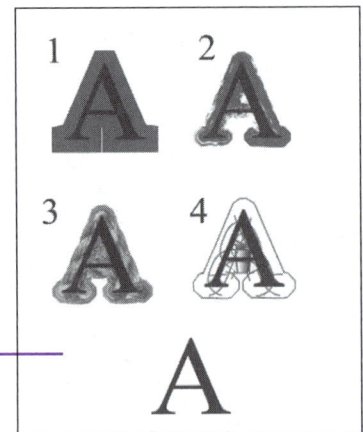

3.2

(T) I P

If you'd like to see more line styles for your outline, click on the Gallery icon at the top of the gallery. The Gallery workpane opens to show more options.

If you want to use a color for the outline that is in another part of the image, click on the Eyedropper tool near the bottom of the Text workpane. Click on the part of the image that contains the color you want to use, and PhotoDraw changes the outline to the color you selected.

3.3

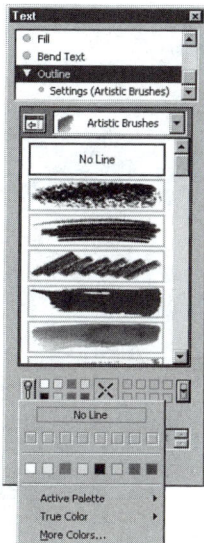

3.4

3. Click on the outline effect you want to use, and PhotoDraw applies the effect.

4. To change the width of the outline, you can either type a point size in the Width box or use the Width slider. You can also click on the up or down arrows next to the Width slider to adjust the width of the outline.

5. If you have chosen a plain or an artistic outline, you can change the color for the outline, by clicking on one of the colored squares at the bottom of the workpane (3.3). PhotoDraw changes the color of the outline to match the one you selected.

6. To access other colors and custom color palettes, click on the arrow button at the right of the color choices. A list of available color palettes appears (3.4).

Ⓝ **O T E**

If you have selected a Photo or Theme brush for your outline, you cannot change the colors in the outline.

Ⓝ **O T E**

If you click on the No Line option, a text object that is not filled with a color will disappear. If the text object is filled with a color, the outline disappears, leaving only the text.

Applying Text Fills

PhotoDraw gives you several ways to fill a text object besides the basic one of changing the color of the fill. Other options include filling the object with a two-color gradient, a texture, a picture, an artistic fill, or a designer gradient.

1. Select the text object you want to change the fill of and open the Text workpane (Format→ Text). Select the Fill option from the list of options at the top of the workpane to view the Fill controls (3.5).

2. Select the type of fill you want to use from the drop-down list of fill types. The workpane changes to show the fill options for that type. Select the option you want to use by clicking on it and PhotoDraw applies the fill effect to the text object.

3. To change a solid fill color, click on the arrow button at the right of the color choices. A list of color palettes appears. Click on the name of the color palette you want to use, and the palette opens to enable you to select the desired color (3.6).

(T) I P

Applying a fill to an object fills the entire object with the chosen fill type, including any outlines you might have added previously. To apply an outline to an object that is different from the fill, add the outline after you have made the fill choice.

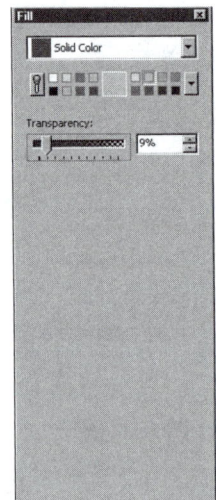

3.5

Use colors from a preselected color scheme to help give business graphics, and logos, or Web graphics a consistent look.

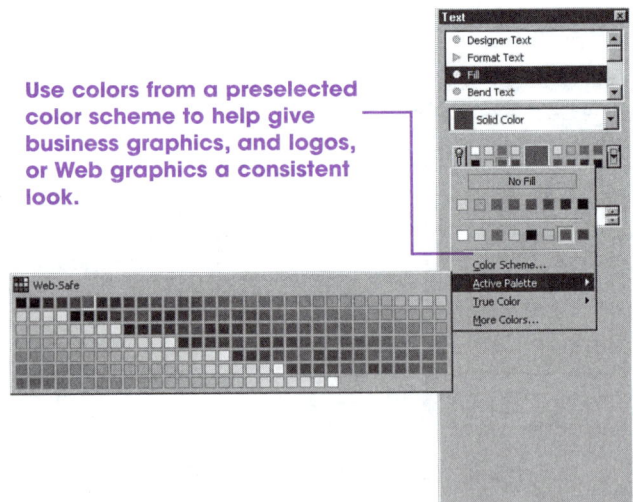

3.6

Changing Texture Fills and Colors

3.7

3.8

To use another texture or image that's on your hard disk but not in the gallery, click on the Browse button and locate the image file you want to use. PhotoDraw uses that file to fill the text object.

You can fill text objects with any one of dozens of ready-to-use textures included with PhotoDraw. You can also change the colors of the textures while keeping the same texture pattern. Another nice feature is that you can also fill the text object with a texture from another program or with an image not included with PhotoDraw's gallery of fills. This enables you to create new text objects that will have the same look as those you might already be using.

1. Select the text object you want to fill with a texture, and select Format→Fill→Texture. The Fill workpane with the gallery of texture fills appears (3.7).

2. Select the fill you want to use by clicking on the fill sample in the gallery. PhotoDraw fills the text object with your selection (3.8).

continues

(T) I P

To make the most of a texture fill, use a "fat" font for your text that has wide characters. That way, more of the texture will be visible.

Changing Texture Fills and Colors continued

3. To change the color of the fill, select a color from the color choices at the bottom of the Fill workpane. You can also use the Eyedropper tool to sample a color from part of another image. PhotoDraw will create a texture fill using the color you have selected.

To make the texture fill lighter or darker, use the Transparency slider tool.

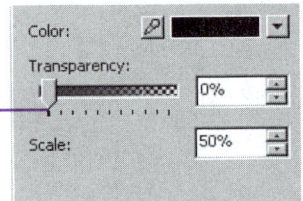

3.9

4. To make the texture of the fill appear more complex, use a percentage figure of less than 100% in the Scaling box. The smaller the number, the smaller the details on the fill **(3.9)**.

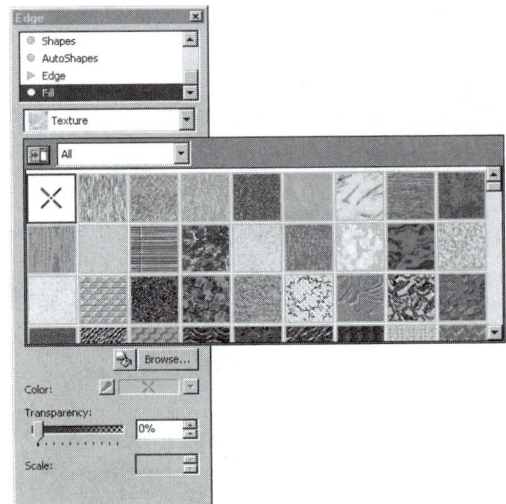

3.10

O T E

You can also use Theme Textures to fill your text objects. Select Format→Fill→Theme Texture to open the Theme workpane. The procedures for applying and changing theme textures work exactly like the procedures described in these steps.

O T E

There are three kinds of texture fills to choose from: Material, Designer, and Theme. Leave the workpane setting on All to have all of the fills show up in one gallery **(3.10)**.

Changing Designer Gradient Fills and Colors

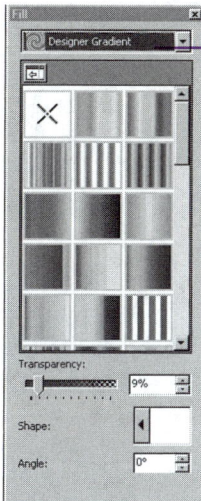

3.11

If you are changing other aspects of the appearance of the text object and already have the Text workpane open, you can select Designer Gradient from the drop-down list.

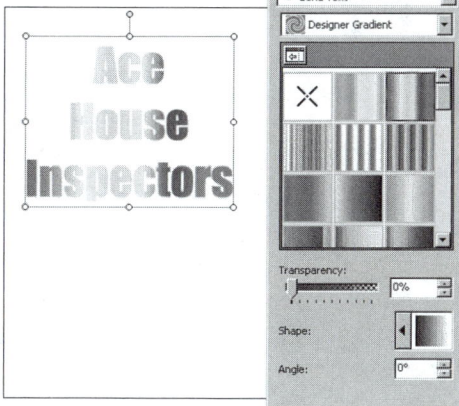

3.12

A gradient is a color ramp made up of more than one color. Designer gradients in PhotoDraw are multi-color fills made of brilliant colors. They are a fun way to add some lively color to a text object.

1. Select the text object you want to fill with a designer gradient, and select Format→Fill→ Designer Gradient. The Fill workpane with the gallery of designer gradient fills appears **(3.11)**.

2. Select the fill you want to use from the gallery by clicking on the fill sample in the gallery. PhotoDraw fills the text object with your selection **(3.12)**.

3. You can change the lightness and darkness of the fill by moving the Transparency slider tool. Move it to the right to make the text look more translucent; move it to the left to make it look more opaque.

continues

(T) I P

You can also type a number for the percentage of transparency you want to use. Typing a number instead of using the slider is a good idea if you want to use the same percentage of transparency in several images.

Changing Designer Gradient Fills and Colors continued

4. To open a gallery of all the different gradient shapes you can apply to the designer gradient, click on the left-pointing arrow in the Shape area to display the shape gallery **(3.13)**. Select the shape you want to use by clicking on it, and PhotoDraw applies the shape to the Designer Fill you applied to the text object.

5. To rotate the fill, enter a number in the Angle box. A positive number rotates the fill clockwise; a negative number rotates it counterclockwise.

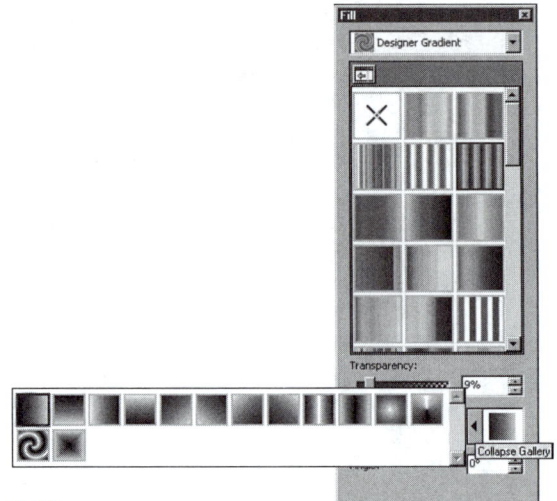

3.13

(N) O T E

Some of the fills do not appear to change much after you've rotated the fill. Changing the shape of the fill makes a more pronounced difference.

Applying Two-Color Gradient Fills and Colors

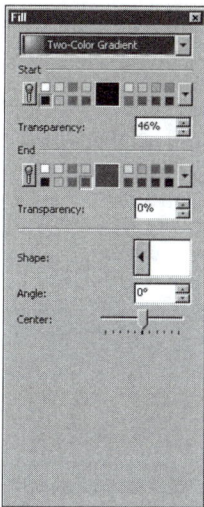

3.14

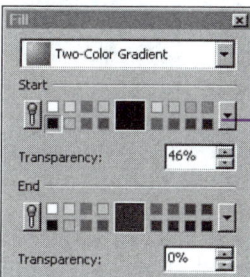

You can also select a color from a color palette by clicking on the down-arrow button and selecting a color from one of the palettes listed.

3.15

Designer gradients are very colorful ways to fill text objects, but for a more subtle look, you might want to use a two-color gradient fill. With a two-color gradient, you can choose the beginning and ending color, plus assign transparency values for each color, as well as the shape and angle for the fill.

1. Select the text object you want to fill with a designer gradient, and select Format→Fill→Two-Color Gradient. The Fill workpane with color-selection palettes for the two-color gradients opens. Two colors for the gradient are already selected (3.14).

2. Select the beginning color for the gradient by clicking on a color shown in the squares in the Start portion of the workpane or by selecting a color using the Eyedropper tool (3.15). PhotoDraw fills the text object with a two-color gradient using the start color you've selected.

3. To change the end color of the gradient, click on a colored square in the End portion of the workpane. You can also select a color from another image by using the Eyedropper tool or from the color palettes, which you can access by clicking on the down-arrow button.

continues

Applying Two-Color Gradient Fills and Colors continued

4. Click on the left arrow next to
Shape to open a gallery of all
the gradient shapes you can
apply to the two-color gradient
(3.16). Select the one you want
to use by clicking on it, and
PhotoDraw applies the shape
to the fill you've chosen for the
text object.

5. To rotate the fill, enter a number in the Angle box. A positive number rotates the fill
clockwise; a negative number
rotates it counterclockwise
(3.17).

3.16   **You can create some wonderful fills with
the two-color gradient fill tools, but you
won't be able to save the fills. So be sure
to write down the settings of fills you like
so that you can re-create them later.**

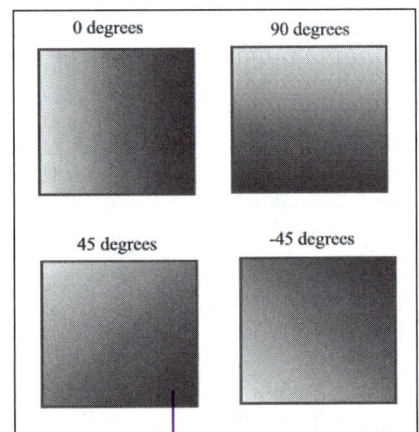

3.17

**In this example, each square was
filled with a two-color gradient
and then the rotation of the fill
was changed as indicated above
each square.**

ⓣ I P

*To achieve a graceful and subtle two-tone
effect for your two-color gradient, select two
shades of the same color for your starting
and ending colors. Be sure to pick shades
with enough range between them to make a
visible shift possible when PhotoDraw cre-
ates the gradient.*

Ⓝ O T E

*To adjust the midpoint of the gradient,
which controls the amount of the starting or
ending color and the in-between mixes of
color in the gradient, use the slider tool next
to the word Center in the Fill workpane.
Slide it to the left to use more of the end
color; slide it to the right to use more of the
start color.*

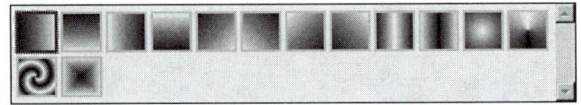

Changing Picture Fills and Colors

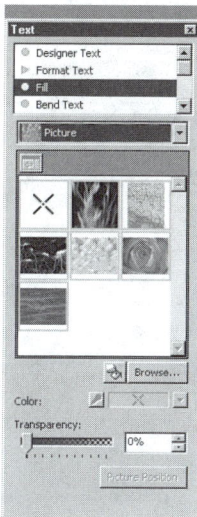

3.18

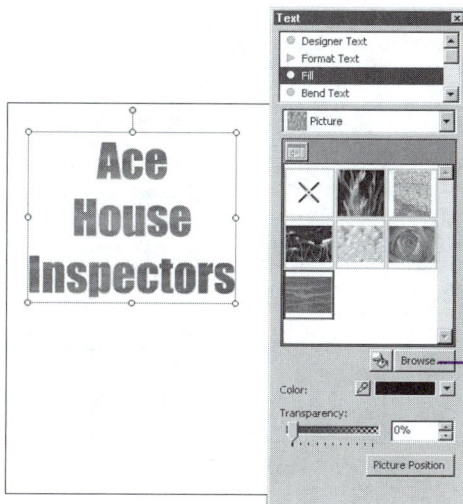

3.19

A picture fill is a very different kind of fill from the others in PhotoDraw. Its closest relative is the texture fill, but you can achieve many more unique fills with a picture fill. Briefly stated, filling a text object with a fill is like making a cutout of the text and placing a picture behind the text. Parts of the picture "show through" the shape of the letters in the text object.

1. Select the text object you want to fill with a picture, and select Format→Fill→Picture. The Fill workpane with the gallery of pictures that can be used as fills appears **(3.18)**.

2. Select the picture you want to use by clicking on the image in the gallery. PhotoDraw fills the text object with your selection **(3.19)**.

You can use another picture for the fill by clicking on the Browse button and selecting an image file or by clicking on the Replace button and then clicking on the image you want to use.

(N) O T E   *continues*

The pictures shown in the fill gallery of picture fills are shown at reduced size. The resulting picture fill from one of these images will not show the same detail in the pictures. Rather, you'll see shapes and colors from the pictures, not specific details.

(T) I P

Using a picture fill is a great way to coordinate the text object with the images in a design or with a theme. For example, you could use photographs of flowers to fill the text object in an ad for a flower shop or landscaping business.

Changing Picture Fills and Colors continued

3. To change the lightness and darkness of the fill after you have applied it, use the Transparency slider to adjust the transparency effect.

4. To change the colors but keep the same general shapes in the fill you've chosen, select a new color by clicking on the down-arrow button next to Color. PhotoDraw uses a range of shades in the new color for the fill but keeps the shape of the fill you chose from the gallery the same.

5. To change which portion of the picture shows in the fill, click on the Picture Position button, and a clear rectangle or square appears onscreen behind the text object **(3.20)**.

6. Adjust the portion of the image "showing through" by clicking on the square or rectangle and moving it around. As you move it around, the fill in the text object changes. When you have found the look you want, click on the Finish button floating above the text object to lock in the position you've chosen **(3.21)**.

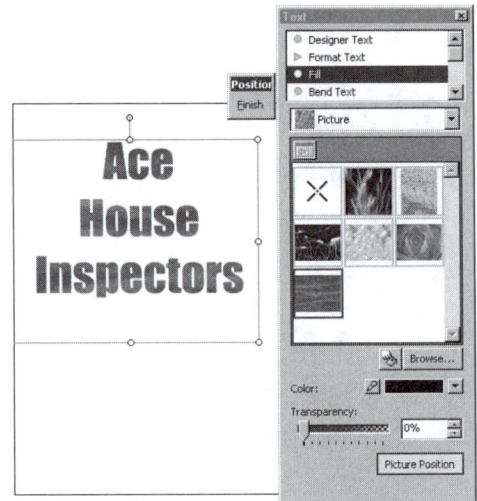

3.20

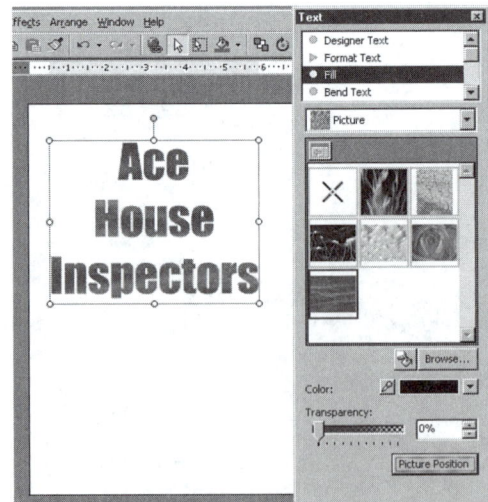

3.21

(N) O T E

You can also select a new color for the fill by using the Eyedropper tool or by accessing the color palettes that pop up after you click on the down-arrow button.

Applying Artistic Fills to Text Objects

3.22

3.23

You can enter a number between 5% and 1000% in the Scale box. The larger the number, the larger the individual pieces of the fill appear.

Of all the fills available in PhotoDraw, the Artistic Fills are the only ones that are only grayscale. They are merely patterns that PhotoDraw fills the object with and then applies the active color to. These fills are mostly subtle effects, so use them when you don't want your text elements to draw a lot of attention. Or use them to coordinate text objects to a textured background.

1. Click on the text object to select it, and open the Artistic Fill workpane (Format→Fill→ Artistic) **(3.22)**.

2. Select a fill from the gallery by clicking on it. PhotoDraw applies the fill to the text object.

3. Change the scale of the fill by typing a new figure in the Scale box on the workpane **(3.23)**. Larger numbers make the individual pieces in the fill appear larger; smaller ones make the pieces shrink.

4. Change the color of the fill by clicking on the down arrow next to the color bar to bring up other color options and selecting a new color.

5. Change the density of the color used in the fill by adjusting the Transparency slider or by typing a new figure in the box next to the slider.

Combining Text Effects

Some of the text effects can be combined to create completely new looks. In this example, a piece of Designer Text has been enhanced via a change of the outline and use of a texture fill to complete the design of the text object. There are many more ways to combine text effects, and experimentation is your best way to learn which effects work best together.

1. Select the Designer Text object you want to add an outline to by clicking on the text object and selecting Format→Text. The Text workpane appears **(3.24)**.

2. Select Fill from the list of options in the Text workpane. Select Texture from the pop-up menu that appears when you click on the down arrow and the gallery of texture fills appears.

3. Select a fill, and PhotoDraw immediately applies it to the text **(3.25)**.

4. To add an outline to the filled text object, select Edge from the list of options in the Text workpane and the gallery of line styles appears. Change the Edge type to Plain by selecting it from the drop-down list of Edge types on the workpane.

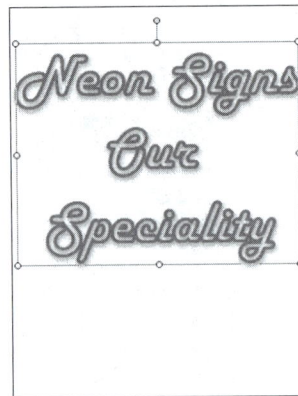

3.24

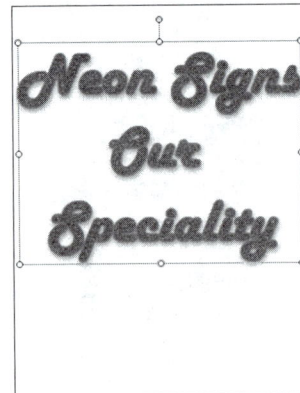

3.25

Be sure that the Transparency percentage is set at 0% before selecting your fill so that you can see the fill you selected as you expected it to look. If the Transparency percentage is higher than 0%, the fill will look lighter or look like a different color than the fill sample shown in the gallery.

3.26

You can change the width of the outline by adjusting the Width slider at the bottom of the workpane.

5. Select the Thick-Thin line style by clicking on it. PhotoDraw applies the style to the text object **(3.26)**.

6. Select the color you want to use for the outline, and PhotoDraw changes the color of the outline to match your selection.

T I P

To give the text object in this example a professional designer touch, use a lighter or darker shade of the main color in the texture fill for the outline color.

CHAPTER 4

Photographs are more and more important to graphic design—especially business-related graphic design—as digital cameras and scanners decrease in price and find their way into businesses. Fortunately, PhotoDraw makes it very easy to incorporate photographic images into your designs and gives you various tools to improve the look of those images.

WORKING WITH PHOTOGRAPHS

To get your original photographs in digital form, you can have someone scan your photographs for you, operate the scanner or collect images from a digital camera yourself, or take advantage of the digital services most photo-labs offer and get a copy of your pictures on a floppy disc or CD-ROM. After you have those images inside PhotoDraw, you can correct image flaws such as scratches, color imbalances, and red eye.

If you want to use stock photography images, they'll already be in digital form and in perfect condition, so you can go directly to the creative tools PhotoDraw gives you for editing photographs. You can also use these tools on original images after you've perfected them.

There are some simple and easy edits you can make, such as copying part of an image or cutting part away. There are more complex edits you can do as well, including merging portions of two or more photographs to make a completely new image and applying special photographic effects.

Acquiring an Image in PhotoDraw

If you have a scanner attached to your computer, you can operate the scanner from inside PhotoDraw. That way, your images come directly into the software, eliminating the extra steps of scanning the image in another program and opening the file inside PhotoDraw later.

1. Choose File→Scan Picture or select Scan Picture from the toolbar to open the Scan workpane (4.1).

2. In the Resolution box, enter a scanning resolution. Choosing the correct resolution depends on the end use of the image. If you're going to be putting it up on a Web site or displaying it on a computer screen, 72dpi is sufficient. However, if you're planning on printing the image, scanning at 150dpi is more appropriate—you'll need the extra detail for a high-quality print.

3. Click Scan and PhotoDraw scans the photograph and opens the image file onscreen (4.2).

To scan the picture without making any adjustments to the brightness, deselect the Auto Brightness/Contrast Correction check box. It's usually preferable to scan the image "as is" and adjust it later in PhotoDraw—you'll have more control this way.

4.1

4.2

You can correct problems with scanned images, such as the scratches and dust marks seen in this scanned image, by following the instructions for those specific tasks found later in this chapter.

(T) I P

If you're not sure what resolution to use, leave the resolution setting on Auto and PhotoDraw will choose a resolution for you.

Erasing Part of a Photograph

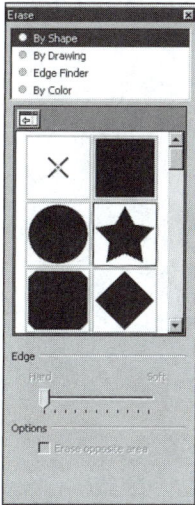

4.3

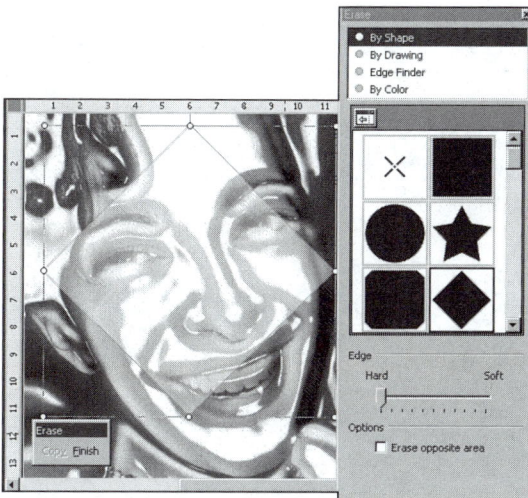

4.4

You might already be familiar with the function of an eraser tool to erase parts of an image from your experience in other software programs. PhotoDraw gives you a set of four Eraser tools that allow you to erase by shape, by drawing freehand, by edge finder, or by color.

With PhotoDraw, you can erase part of an image freehand by drawing a rough outline around the part of the image you want to get rid of. Another of the options is to erase elements by picking out a color or two you want to erase. These methods are best used for erasing elements that are distinctly different from the rest of the image.

Erasing using a shape, outlined as follows, is a simple and precise way to erase part of an image.

1. Open the file you want to erase part of and select Tools→Erase. The Erase workpane appears **(4.3)**.

2. Select By Shape from the list in the workpane.

3. Select a shape for the area you want to erase by clicking on the shape in the workpane. The cursor changes into a cross shape. Click in the image and drag to create the eraser shape **(4.4)**.

continues

Erasing Part of a Photograph continued

4. Click on one of the small circles on the edges of the shape, and drag to adjust the size of the shape to cover just the area you want to erase [**4.5**].

5. Click the Finish button in the Erase floating toolbar. PhotoDraw erases the area within the shape (**4.6**).

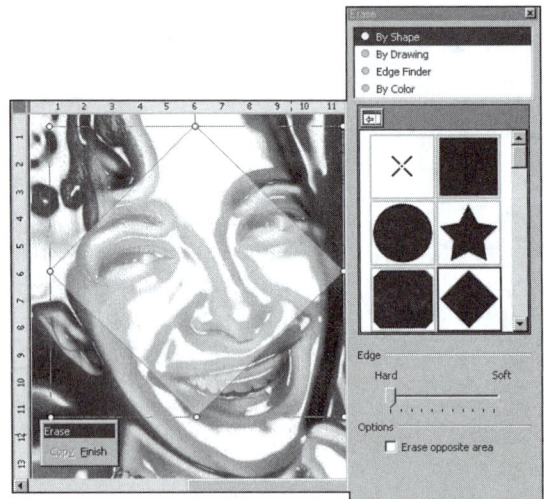

4.5

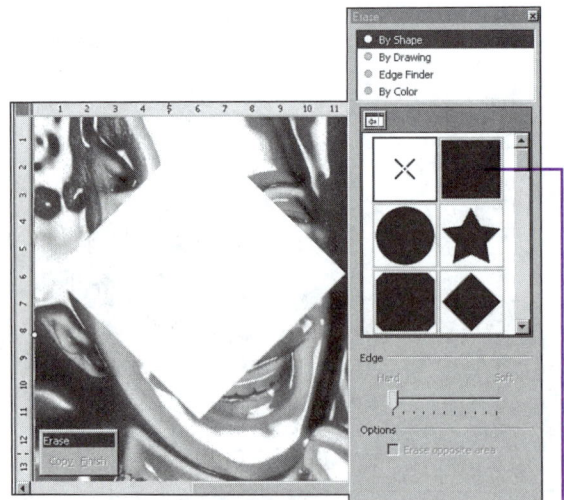

4.6

Don't limit yourself to using just the circle or square cutout shapes. Experiment with some of the more unusual shapes, such as the apple and stamp ones.

(T) I P

To remove an erasing-shape choice before you erase, click on the large ×, which is the first selection in the gallery of shapes.

Cropping a Photograph

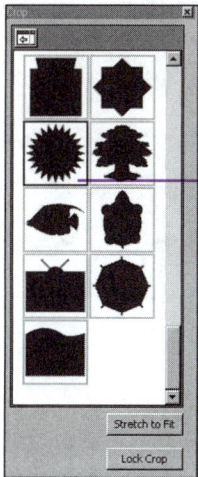

Using the crop function cuts away every part of the image not covered by the shape.

4.7

4.8

Repeat steps 2 through 5 if you want to add additional crops to come up with a combination of cropping shapes.

Cropping in PhotoDraw is done using shapes in much the same way as erasing a portion of an image using a shape is done. The tools used to crop a photograph are the same as those used to erase part of it, but when you crop part of an image, the area inside the shape remains while the rest of the image is removed. Cropping is a good way to get a precisely shaped clip of a photograph or to fit a photograph to a certain-sized frame.

1. Select Tools→Crop by Shape and the Crop workpane appears (4.7).

2. Select the shape you want to crop from the image by clicking on one of the shapes in the workpane. Click on the image and the crop shape appears over the image. The image itself is grayed out slightly.

3. Size the shape so that it covers just the area you want to keep (4.8). If you want the shape to expand to cover the entire image, click the Stretch to Fit button at the bottom of the workpane.

continues

(T) I P

Be sure to save a copy of the original image before you start cropping in case you want start over again or use the entire image for another purpose.

4. Click the Lock Crop button at the bottom of the workpane when you have your crop sized and located where you want to crop.

5. To finish the crop, click the Finish button in the Crop floating toolbar. PhotoDraw deletes the portion of the photograph not covered by the shape, leaving the portion under the shape intact **(4.9)**.

4.9

(T) I P

If you want to crop an irregular shape from a photograph or use color to guide the crop, use the Erase tool and select Erase Opposite Area under the Options section of the Erase workpane.

Cloning Part of a Photograph

4.10

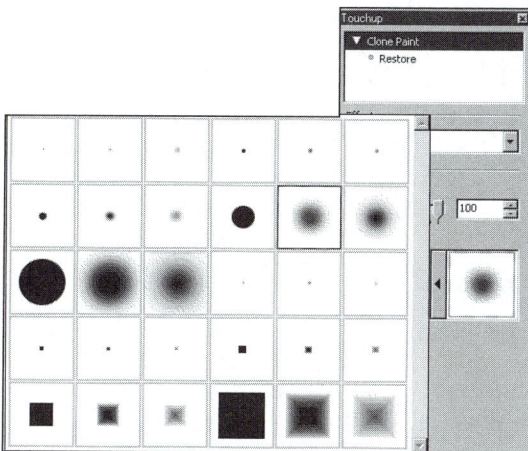

4.11

In PhotoDraw, when you clone part of a photograph, you are actually taking part of an image to use as fill for a digital paintbrush. The sample you take from the image becomes "paint" you can use to alter the appearance of the same, or another, image. It's a good way to take a portion of an image and use it somewhere else, as you might if you could cut and paste only a portion of an image.

1. With your image open, select Format→Touch Up→Select Clone, and the Touchup workpane appears (4.10).

2. Select the amount of the transparency you want in the clone effect by moving the Amount slider in the workpane.

3. Select a brush for the clone paint by clicking on a brush size/shape in the pop-up Brush gallery (4.11).

4. Click near the middle of the area you want to use for clone paint.

continues

(T) I P

Cloning is a good way to develop unique colors for painting an image. A clone paint can be used on any object in PhotoDraw.

Cloning Part of a Photograph continued

5. Move the cursor to the area you want to paint with the clone, and then, holding the mouse button, drag the cursor to paint the area.

6. Click Finish on the floating toolbar when you are finished painting **(4.12)**.

You can see that in this example the subject's left eye was used as the clone paint and was "painted" onto her forehead. Using this feature, you can create some elaborate "Picasso"-type images with just a few clicks.

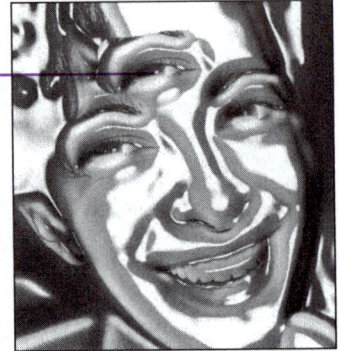

4.12

(N) O T E

You can restore the image to its original appearance by clicking on the Restore button in the floating toolbar.

(N) O T E

If the cloning feature doesn't do the trick for you, try cropping to the desired part of the image and then copying and pasting it into another image window containing the image you want to add a "clone" to.

Merging Parts of Photographs

4.13

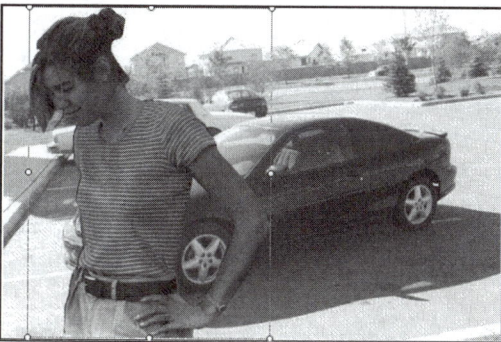

4.14

Sometimes, you won't find the precise image you're looking for in your photographs, but you could make exactly what you want by combining portions of two or more photographs. With a little practice, you'll be so good at doing this that no one will be able to tell that you pieced the image together.

1. Open the files containing the images you want to use parts of (4.13), or place all of the images in one workspace.

2. Crop the portions of the images you want to use. Cropping removes portions of the image, so if you plan to reuse the original image, either do not save the cropped image or save it under another name to keep the original intact.

3. Size the portions so that they are in proper proportion to each other (4.14).

continues

Merging Parts of Photographs continued

4. Arrange the image portions in the new design to fit your needs **(4.15)**. You can use the alignment features in the Arrange→Align menu to help you get things lined up on the page the way you want them.

5. Group the images (Arrange→Group) to ensure that the arrangement you've chosen remains in place.

6. Save the new image **(4.16)**.

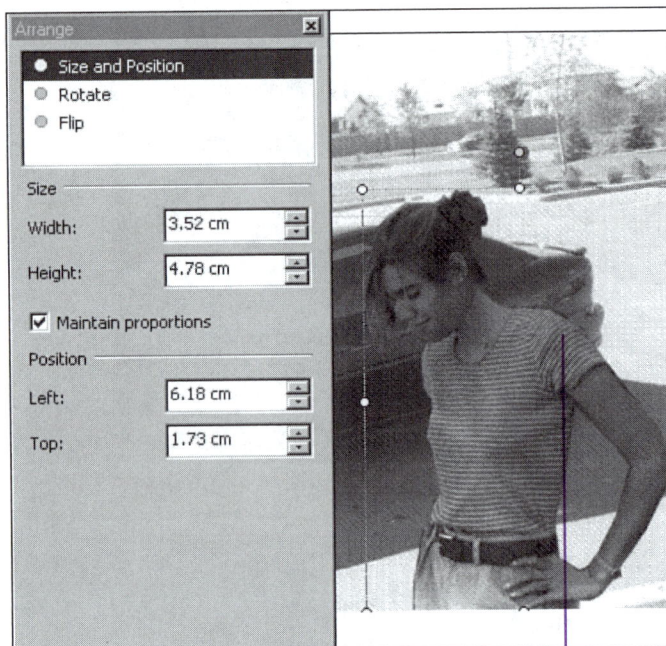

4.15

When you arrange the items, be sure to layer them if needed to give the image a feeling of depth.

(N) O T E

Unless you're experienced at making irregular crops, don't try to combine elements of different pictures unless you can use the cropping shapes. It's difficult in irregular crops to get close enough to the portion of the image you want to use without snipping out important bits—and the edges of your images will look like paper dolls cut out with old, blunt scissors.

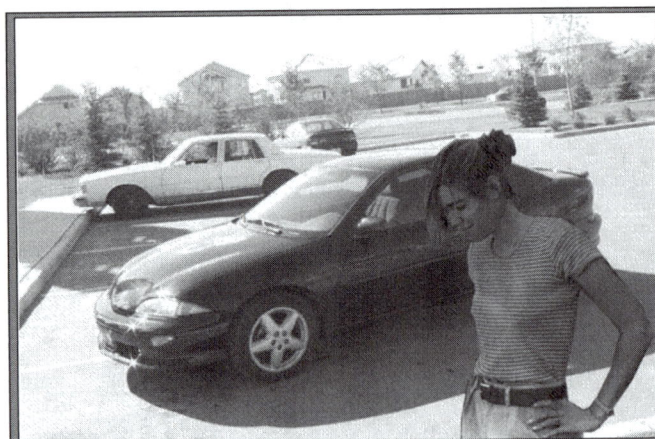

4.16

Correcting and Balancing Colors

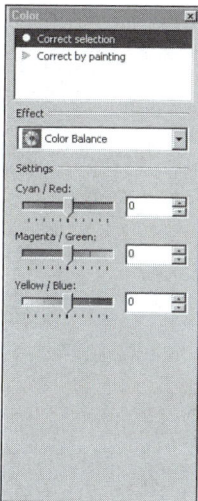

4.17

If there's a greenish hue in your image (sometimes from indoor lighting), move the Magenta/Green slider to –3 and watch the effect—your image will be warmer. Experiment and feel free to get creative. You can create some wonderful effects by saturating an image with certain colors.

4.18 **Moving a slider to the left adds more of the first color in the group to the image. Moving it to the right adds more of the second.**

Knowing how to correct and balance colors in a photograph will allow you to use images you might otherwise have to discard. Unfortunately, even with professional photographs, you will often need to make changes in the color balance of the image. You are more likely to need to make such changes in photographs that were not taken by a professional or that were not scanned correctly.

1. Open the photographic image you want to edit, and click on it to select it.

2. Select Format→Color→Color Balance and the Color workpane appears (4.17).

3. Adjust the amount of Cyan/Red, Magenta/Green, and Yellow/Blue in the picture by moving the slider in the workpane or by typing a number in the box next to the slider (4.18). Visual cues are the best way to adjust this—how do you want the image to look? Try different combinations of settings until you get the look you want.

(N)O T E

Another way to adjust the color in a photograph is to adjust the tint. Select your object, and then choose Format→Touchup→Correct Tint. Use the Automatic button to make quick corrections.

Adjusting Brightness and Contrast

Adjusting the brightness and contrast in a photograph is one of the most common changes you'll have to make when working with photographic images. Sometimes, the image is so dark or light that it will not reproduce well when photocopied or printed. Adjusting these two elements of a picture can sometimes correct problems in the original image so that you can use the digital version without concern.

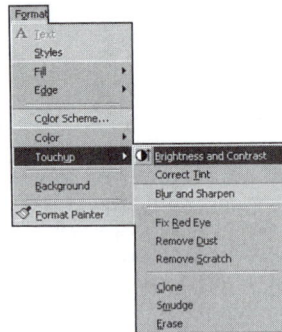

4.19

1. Open the photographic image you want to correct, and click on it to select it.

2. Select Format→Touchup, and the pop-up list of image-editing options opens (4.19).

3. Select Brightness and Contrast from the menu, and the Color workpane opens with the brightness and contrast controls (4.20). Moving the Brightness slider to the left darkens the image; sliding it to the right makes it brighter.

4.20   **To heighten the contrast and bring out more details, move the Contrast slider to the right. Sliding it to the left makes the image look flatter because the amount of contrast between elements in the image is lessened.**

Ⓝ O T E

Be careful not to overdo the adjustments to brightness and contrast. Your particular monitor settings will be different from other users', so what looks dark to you may be bright to others. It's best to set your monitor controls to a neutral setting. If this image is for printing, do a test printout to see how your printer handles the image—you will need to adjust it based on what you see on the printed page rather than what's on your screen.

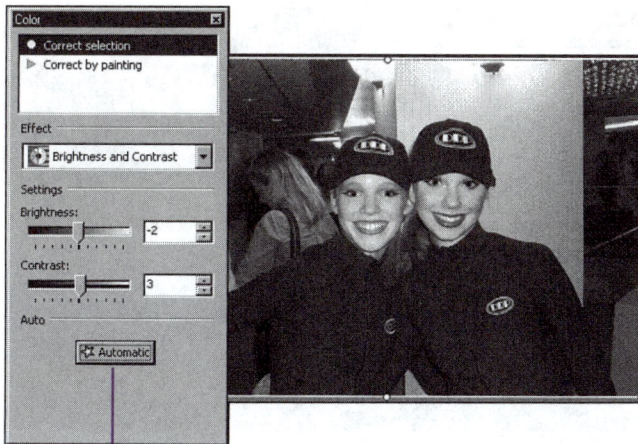

4.21

When you press the Automatic button, PhotoDraw will analyze the image and determine the optimal value for brightness and contrast. It's usually quite accurate, but you might need to adjust the values slightly depending on the final use of your image.

4. If you want PhotoDraw to automatically make the decisions about how to correct the brightness and contrast of the image, click on the Automatic button at the bottom of the workpane.

5. If you want to make the brightness and contrast adjustments manually, move the sliders or type a number in the boxes until you are satisfied with the result (4.21).

(T) I P

Use the automatic adjustment unless you want to change the brightness or contrast for a specific printing application (such as making an image have more contrast because you know that it will be photocopied) or to achieve a special effect.

(N) O T E

You can change the brightness and contrast settings of a group of photographic images by selecting them all before changing the brightness or contrast controls.

Removing Red Eye

Red eye is that unfortunate problem in photographs that makes people and animals look slightly demonic due to the red in their eyes where more seemly colors such as blue and brown should appear. You won't find it in professional photographs or stock photography, but you might find it popping up in other photographs. Fortunately, PhotoDraw gives you two ways to remove red eye from a photograph: an automatic method and a manual method.

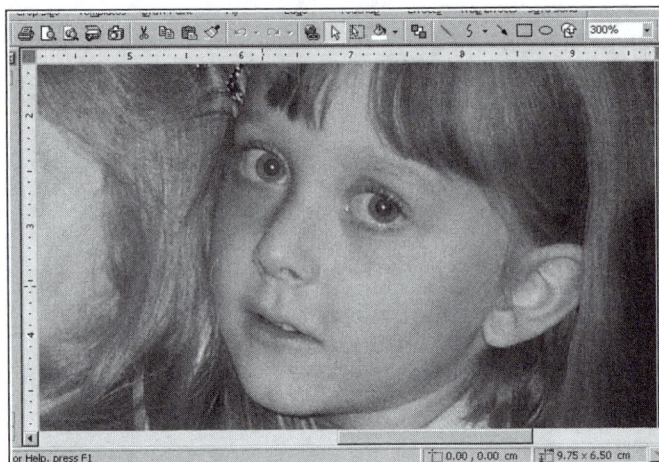

4.22

Use the automatic correction method unless there is considerable detail in the eye area that you want to retain when the red eye is removed. If that is the case, use the manual method for more control over the process.

1. To use the automatic red-eye removal option, first open the image and zoom in to enlarge the area with the problem **(4.22)**.

(T) I P

Be sure to enlarge the image by typing a number in the Zoom box on the right side of the toolbar. Make the number high enough that you can click on the area in the eye where the red is and not the area that is colored correctly. If you don't, you might end up changing too much of the eye's appearance.

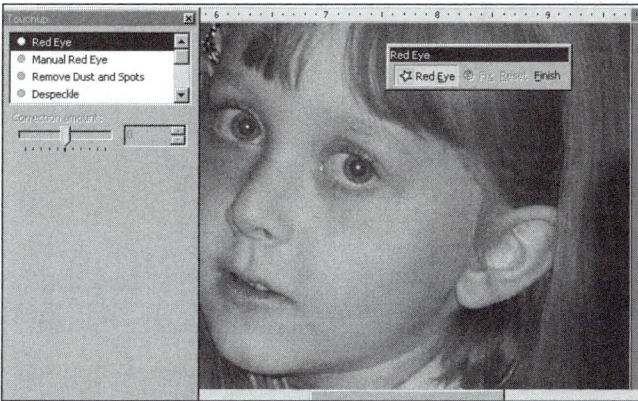

4.23

4.24   **The final image is corrected and no longer has the red-eye problem, resulting in a much more pleasing photograph.**

2. Select Format→Touch Up→Fix Red Eye, and the Touchup workpane appears with Red Eye selected on the list of options. (For instructions on the manual correction process, skip to step 6.)

3. Click on the pupils of the eyes you want to remove the red eye from to select them, one face at a time **(4.23)**.

4. Click Fix on the Red Eye floating toolbar, and PhotoDraw corrects the red-eye problem **(4.24)**.

5. If you can still see red in the eyes, adjust the amount of red-eye correction by moving the Correction Amount slider until you are satisfied with the result.

continues

(T) I P

PhotoDraw replaces the red in the eyes by copying and pasting the eye color around the red portion. Be careful to click only in the center of the eye area to avoid changing the white portion of the eye.

Removing Red Eye continued

6. To correct the red-eye problem manually, select Manual Red Eye from the list of touchup options. The floating toolbar changes to the Manual Red Eye toolbar **(4.25)**.

7. Select one eye to correct, and click to start the first selection on the outside of the affected area.

8. Click and drag to outline the area to be corrected. As you click and drag, a line appears **(4.26)**. When you are finished, click to stop drawing.

9. Click the Fix button on the floating toolbar. Then click Finish when you've finished dealing with the red-eye problem.

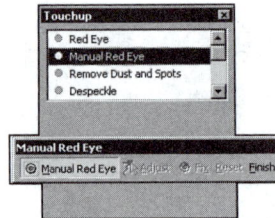

4.25

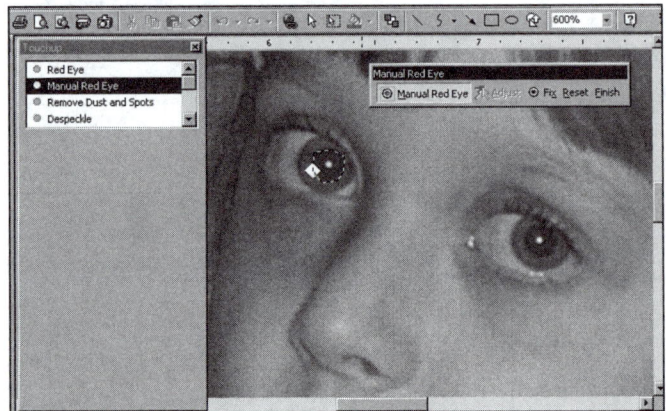

4.26

(N) O T E

To adjust the line you've drawn to select an area, click on the Adjust button on the floating toolbar and resize the outline so that it fits the area better.

(N) O T E

An alternative way of fixing the red-eye problem is to actually paint over it with PhotoDraw's painting tools. Using standard black will do the trick, but using a different color (white, yellow, and so on) can have an eerie effect on the image!

Fixing Scratches and Other Image Problems

4.27

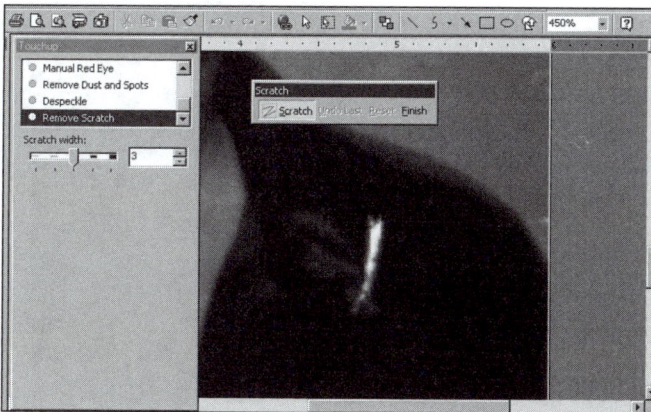

4.28

Sometimes, a photograph is damaged in some way because it has been mishandled or because it is old. It might have been scratched, bent, or allowed to wrinkle. Or, the scan of a photograph might be marred by dust spots. You can correct these imperfections, along with a few other image problems, by using the image-correction tools in PhotoDraw.

1. To remove a scratch from a scan of a photograph, open the image file (4.27) and zoom in so that you can see the beginning and end of the scratch.

2. Select FormatfiTouch Up→Remove Scratch, and the Touchup workpane opens with Remove Scratch highlighted (4.28).

continues

T I P

You can use the same method for removing scratches to fix other visual defects in an image. For example, you can remove the lines from around someone's eyes by using this method.

Fixing Scratches and Other Image Problems continued

3. Click on the beginning of the scratch and then, following the line of the scratch, move to the end slowly and click again. PhotoDraw draws a colored line over the scratch **(4.29)**. When you finish drawing and click the Finish button, PhotoDraw removes the line and the scratch automatically.

4. To remove small flaws and spots, select Format→Touch Up→Remove Dust, and the Touchup workpane appears with Remove Dust and Spots highlighted.

5. Click on each of the dust spots or flaws you want removed.

6. Click the Finish button on the Dust and Spots floating toolbar to remove the flaws **(4.30)**.

(N) O T E

If your image has a few small flaws or dust specs, you can remove them one by one or you can remove them all at once. If you need to remove more than four or five small spots, it's faster to remove all of them at once.

(T) I P

Use the despeckle option to remove multiple small flaws or wrinkles from a picture. The image might look slightly blurry afterward **(4.31)***; if so, sharpening the image will bring back some of the detail.*

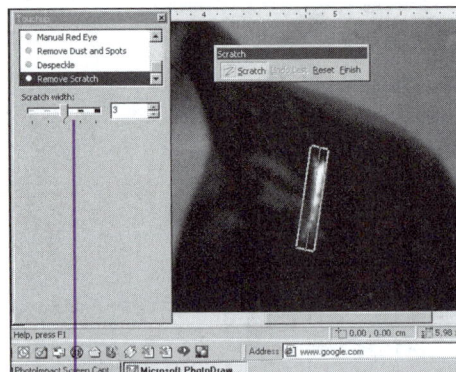

4.29 └ **You can adjust the width of the scratch remover to fit the width of the scratch. That way, you're not editing more of the image than you have to.**

4.30

A before and after shot of a photo with severe scratching and spotting. Using the Remove Scratch and Remove Dust and Spots, the flaws can be cleaned up. Following up with a mild sharpening brings back the clarity of the image.

4.31

Applying Photographic Special Effects

4.32   **If you want to narrow your list of effect choices, select a category from the work-pane drop-down list.**

In addition to the basic photographic editing tools covered earlier in this chapter, PhotoDraw provides some cool special effects you can apply to photographs. These effects can be applied to all images in PhotoDraw, including clip art and text objects; however, when applied to photographic images, they instantly transform a photograph into a dramatically different-looking image. You can even make a photograph look like a watercolor or an oil painting.

1. Open the file containing the photograph (or object) you want to apply the special effect to, and click on the item to select it.

2. Select Effects→Designer Effects and the Designer Effects workpane with the gallery of designer effects appears (4.32).

continues

(T) I P

Using these designer effects on photographs gives you many ways to use the same image. All you need to do is pick a designer effect in keeping with the style of the rest of the design, and you can create a different-looking image every time.

Applying Photographic Special Effects continued

3. Scroll through the list of designer effects and choose one by clicking on the thumbnail example of the effect; PhotoDraw then applies the effect **(4.33)**.

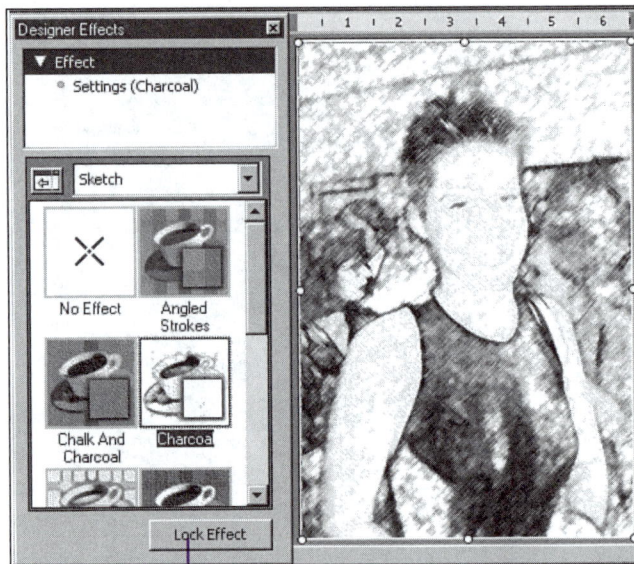

4.33   **To lock the effect so that you can finish or to combine that effect with others, click on the Lock Effect button at the bottom of the workpane.**

(T) I P

Certain effects are quite harsh in their default values, but there's an easy way to create a beautiful blend of the new and old image. By going into settings, you can adjust the transparency value—this is the amount of the old image that shows through. At a 50% transparency, you can see most of the original image, but it's overlaid with the new effect, creating an incredible effect **(4.34)**! *Experiment with the transparency slider and other options on the settings tab.*

(N) O T E

Remember that you can combine special effects or apply special effects to a cropped portion of an image and then combine the portions and apply a special effect to a group of images.

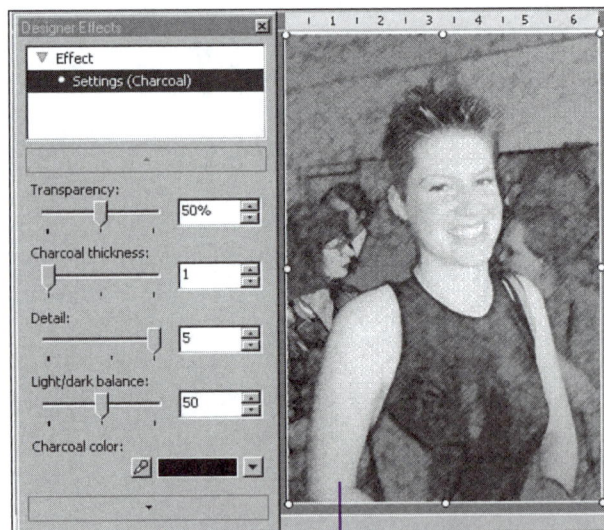

4.34   **This is the same image with the charcoal effect applied to it, only the transparency is set to 50%, resulting in a more moderate effect, and an overall more pleasing image.**

Changing the Default Picture Quality

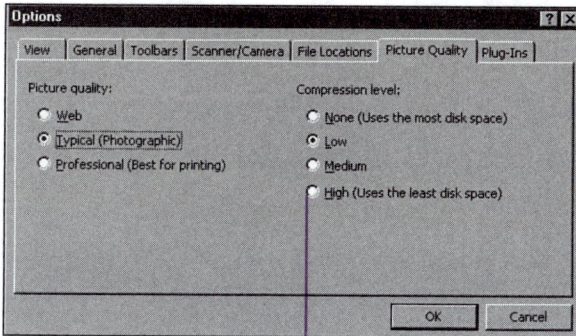

4.35 **Selecting high levels of compression makes file sizes smaller but also reduces image quality, so don't use a setting lower than Medium unless you really need to conserve disk space.**

You should know how to change the default print-quality settings in PhotoDraw and should keep those settings in mind as you work with photographic images. Keep the setting on the default of Typical (Photographic) unless you work with images that will be used only onscreen (Web sites, PowerPoint, and so on), in which case you should use the Web setting. You should use the Professional setting if your photographic images will be printed by a professional printer or you have a high-resolution printer to output your images on (600+dpi).

1. Open the picture-quality controls by selecting Tools→ Options and clicking on the Picture Quality tab (4.35).

2. Select the picture quality and the compression level you want to use.

3. Click OK to save the setting changes.

(N) O T E

After saving a picture with the Web setting, you can't improve the image quality by selecting one of the other two settings. The same is true if the original image was scanned at a low resolution.

Batch Processing Photographic Images

PhotoDraw lets you apply several photographic imaging processes to a group of images in a batch process. Simply select the images you want to process, choose the changes you want to make, and PhotoDraw applies those changes automatically. You can change file formats, picture size, color depth, and resolution by using the batch process.

1. Select File→Batch Save to activate the Batch Save Wizard (4.36).

2. To process all currently open pictures, click the first option, All Open Pictures. To process only a few you select, click the middle option. To process all images in a specific folder, click the last option.

3. Click the Next button and enter the information about where PhotoDraw should save the edited files and about the file format you want to use (4.37).

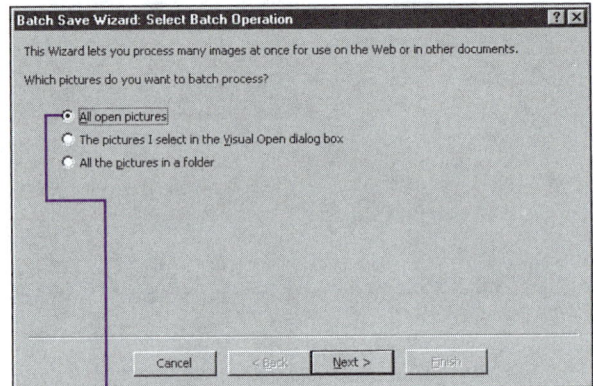

4.36   **You can choose to process all open files, only files you select, or files you've copied into one folder.**

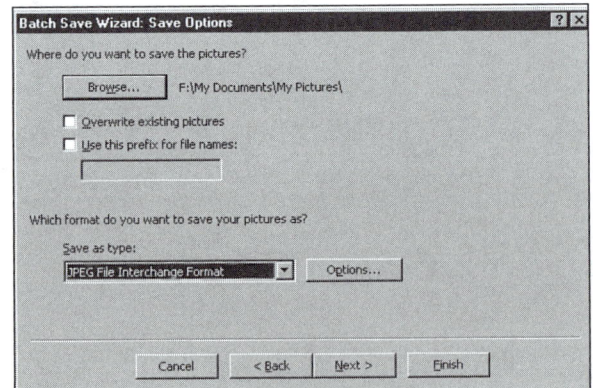

4.37

(T) I P

Using the batch process comes in handy whenever you have more than one or two images to edit in one or more of these ways, so it's a good procedure to learn and remember to use. It's especially useful for creating Web-based photo albums. If you have dozens of images taken with a digital camera or scanned, you'll need to resize them and save them as compressed JPEG images. The batch save is your ticket to saving time!

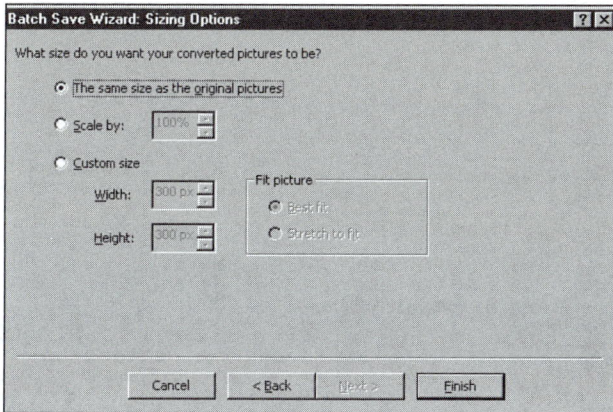

Batch Save Wizard: Sizing Options

What size do you want your converted pictures to be?

- ⊙ The same size as the original pictures
- ○ Scale by: 100%
- ○ Custom size
    - Width: 300 px
    - Height: 300 px

Fit picture
- ⊙ Best fit
- ○ Stretch to fit

[Cancel]   [< Back]   [Next >]   [Finish]

4.38

4. Click the Next button and choose the size you want the edited images to be **(4.38)**.

5. Click the Finish button to make PhotoDraw start the batch-editing process.

Ⓝ **O T E**

If you have asked PhotoDraw to process more than a few images or the images are large files, the batch processing can take several minutes or even hours.

CHAPTER 5

In this chapter you will learn how to...

Open and Use a Template

Use Designer Edges Templates

Use Designer Clip Art Templates

Create a Custom Logo

Customize a Flyer

Maximize Web Graphics Templates

Create a Business Card from a Template

Create a PowerPoint Background from a Template

PhotoDraw templates can give you a professional-looking design with a very small investment in time and effort. The templates are broken down into five main categories:

- Web Graphics—Includes advertising banners, site banners, navigation buttons, sidebars, buttons (circular, connecting, festive, rectangular), and backgrounds.

USING TEMPLATES TO CREATE IMAGES

- Theme Graphics—An assortment of graphic templates to match themes common to other Microsoft Products (Publisher, PowerPoint, and so on). The Web-site graphic templates in this area are completely different from the Web Graphics templates, giving you even more variety.

- Business Graphics—Nearly 100 templates occupy this area, covering certificates, flyers, frames, address labels, decorative labels, round labels, shipping labels, logos, portfolio pages, PowerPoint backgrounds, PowerPoint bullets, retail (point of purchase designs), and signs.

- Cards—Announcements, greeting cards, postcards, and tent cards are available in this template area.

- Designer Clip Art—More than 200 clip art images from 13 categories.

Each template is a design wizard that takes you through a step-by-step customization process. You can change some of the graphics and the text in a template as you follow along with the wizard. After that process is complete, you can customize the design even further using all the tools PhotoDraw offers.

Opening and Using a Template

1. Select File→New from Template. The Templates workpane opens, displaying the available categories in the template gallery (5.1).

2. Select the type of template you want to use from the drop-down list of options in the workpane (5.2).

3. Double-click on one of the thumbnails of template styles in the workspace. PhotoDraw opens that design file in the workspace, and the workpane advances to the next step (5.3).

4. If you want to use the image in the template as it is shown, click the Next button at the bottom of the workpane. If not, follow the wizard's instructions to replace the picture with another one. When finished, click the Next button to proceed.

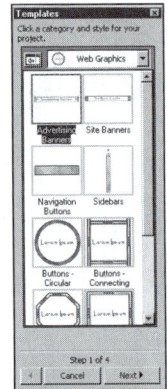

5.1

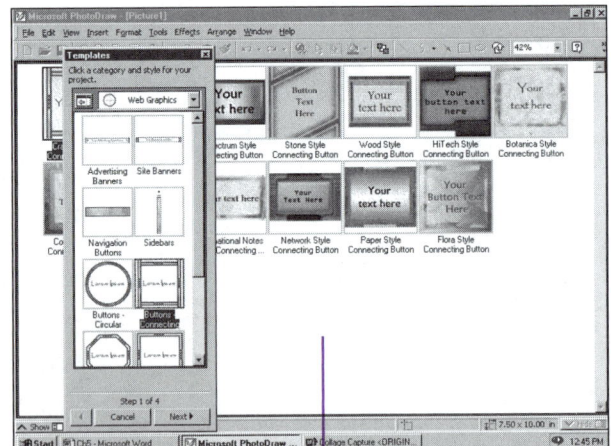

5.2 **When you select a category of templates, thumbnails of the styles of designs in that category appear in the workspace behind the workpane.**

Click the Picture Position button to move the picture from the default position. Move the picture to the new position, and click the Finish button on the floating workpane.

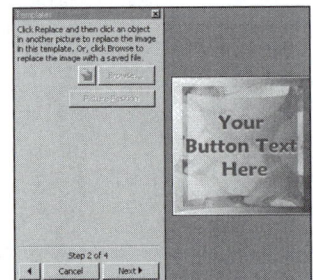

5.3

(T) I P

Move the workpane out of the way of the template before you begin making changes so that you can see the whole template while you're working.

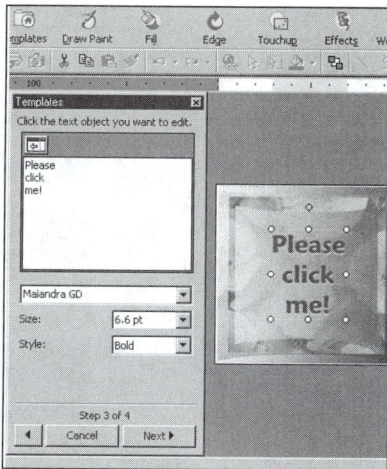

5.4

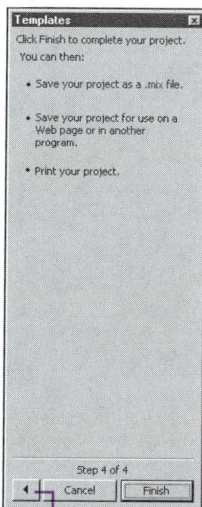

5.5 If you would like to make changes to any part of the template, click the left-arrow button to return to previous steps.

5. You can edit the wording of the text, and change the font size, style and font selection at this step **(5.4)**. Click the Next button to continue.

6. Review the template and click the Finish button to complete the design **(5.5)**.

NOTE

Not all the templates take you step-by-step through changing every element of a template, including editing text. After you create a design from such a template, you can go back and make additional changes as you would in any of your own designs.

Using Designer Edges Templates

You've seen the fancy edging and framing effects on images in magazines, in newspapers, and even on T-shirts. You can buy plug-ins to create these special effects, or you can use the Designer Edges templates to create them.

1. First open the file that has the image you want to add the designer edge to. Then, select Format→Edge→Designer Edges to open the Designer Edges workpane.

2. Select the type of edge from the drop-down list of template types. The workpane changes to show the selection of edges in that category (5.6).

You have three types of Designer Edges to choose from: Artistic, Paper, and Traditional.

5.6

(N) O T E

PhotoDraw offers dozens of edge designs in each category. Because each design can be customized in various ways, you can design hundreds of edges for your images.

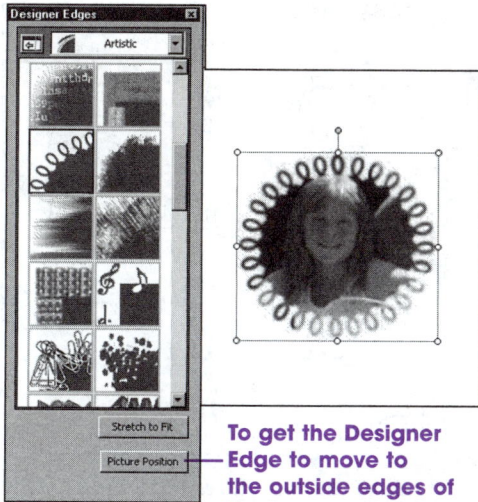

5.7

To get the Designer Edge to move to the outside edges of the image, click the Stretch to Fit button.

3. Click on the type of Designer Edge you want to use by clicking on the thumbnail example. PhotoDraw applies the edging effect to the image **(5.7)**.

4. To move the image around within the frame you've created with the Designer Edge, click the Picture Position button and click on the image. Hold the mouse button down and slide the image around until you are satisfied with the look. Click Finish on the floating toolbar to end the editing.

(T) I P

Be sure that you have completed all image edits or photographic corrections needed before you apply the edge. Effects applied later will be made to the frame in addition to the image underneath.

(N) O T E

For a very special and artistic look, you can apply edges on top of edges by replacing the image under an edge with an image that already has a designer edge.

Using Designer Clip Art Templates

If you've ever thought that a piece of clip art would work well in one of your designs if only you could change it a little, you'll be happy to know that Designer Clip Art templates help you do that. Using the templates, you select a basic black-and-white line-art type of clip art image from the Clip Gallery, and the wizard walks you through a quick method of changing the clip art. After you've completed the Design Wizard process, you can continue to customize the image using the rest of PhotoDraw's image-editing capabilities.

1. Select File→New from Template and the Templates workpane opens.

2. Select Designer Clip Art from the list of templates in the workpane to open the gallery of clip art categories (5.8).

3. Select one of the pieces of clip art to customize by clicking on the thumbnail of the clip art image. Then, click the Next button. The Artistic Brushes gallery opens in the Templates workpane.

4. Customize the clip art image by changing the type, size, and color of the brush (5.9). Click the Next button and then the Finish button when you have finished making changes.

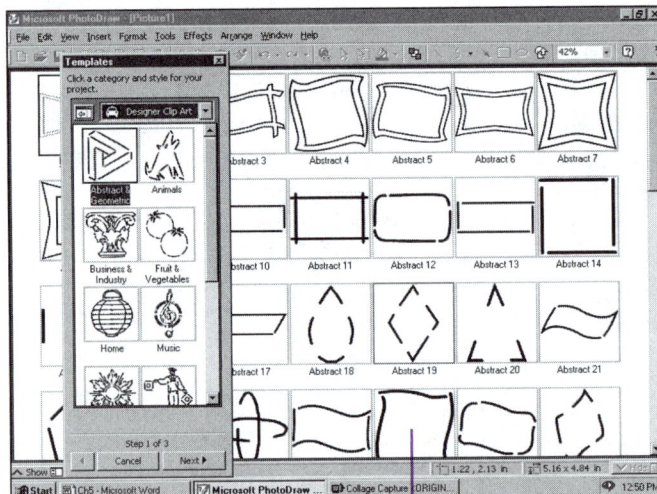

5.8   **Whenever you open a template workpane and select a category of templates, PhotoDraw automatically opens the gallery and selects the items in one type of template to display in the workspace behind the workpane.**

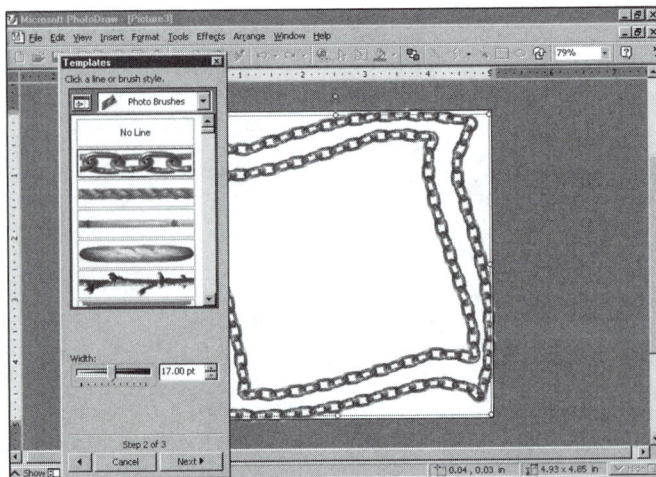

5.9   **Change the width of the effect by moving the Width slider or entering a point size in the box. The default value of 1 point is too fine for most clip art. Try values between 2.0 and 7.0 for the best results.**

Creating a Custom Logo

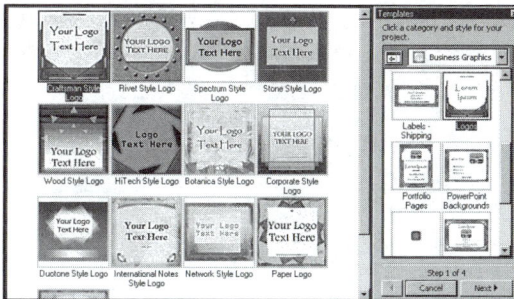

5.10

Many of the logos in the icon templates could be used on business cards, Web sites, and even small posters.

5.11

5.12

If you're in need of a custom logo for your company or project, PhotoDraw has an assortment of 13 different logo designs. Not a large assortment, but with creative use of the various tools, you can create a unique logo with relatively little effort.

1. Create the logo first by selecting File→New from Template and selecting Business Graphics from the list of templates.

2. Select Logos from the gallery of business graphics types by clicking on the Logos icon. The logo styles appear in the workspace behind the workpane (5.10).

3. Double-click on the logo style you want to customize. PhotoDraw moves to the next step in the process and displays the logo in the workspace (5.11).

4. Replace the picture in the logo and click the Next button (5.12).

5. On the next workpane, change the text in the logo and format it as desired. Click the Next button to go to the next step, and click the Finish button to complete this part of the process.

Customizing a Flyer

The Business Graphics category of templates contains templates for many kinds of business-related publications and designs, including flyers, bulletins, labels, logos, and even PowerPoint bullets. You can use the templates as they are or further customize them by including customized elements. This task will take you through the process of customizing a flyer to get you familiar with the process so that you can go on to work with any of the available templates in the same way.

1. Start the Flyer Wizard by selecting File→New from Template and selecting Business Graphics from the list of templates. Select a flyer style to customize by double-clicking one (5.13).

2. In Step 2 of the wizard, you can replace the picture with a customized logo you've created (or with another image) by clicking on the image to be replaced and then clicking the Browse button to locate the customized logo.

3. Adjust the position of the logo as needed by using the Picture Position button. After the logo is in place, click the Next button to move to the next step.

4. Edit the text as needed. Click the Finish button to stop using the wizard (5.14).

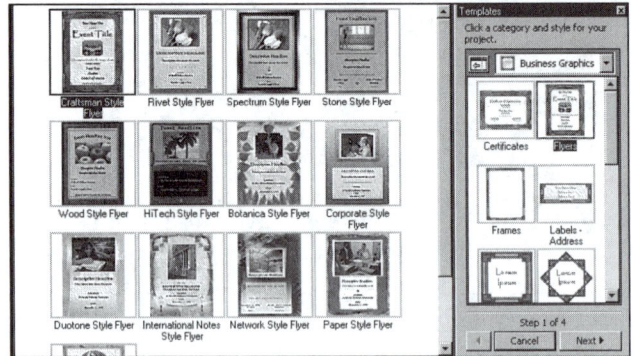

5.13

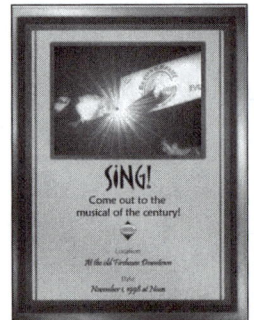

5.14

Maximizing Web Graphics Templates

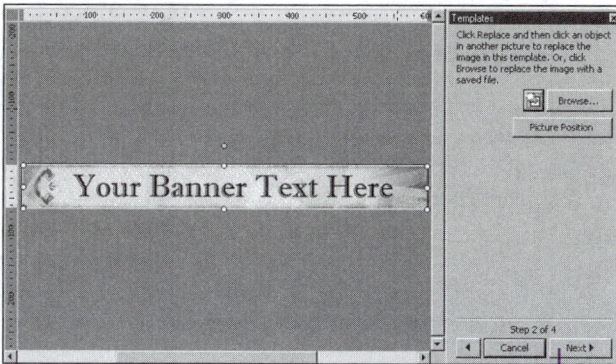

5.15

Move through the wizard by clicking the Next button and following the instructions for customizing the template.

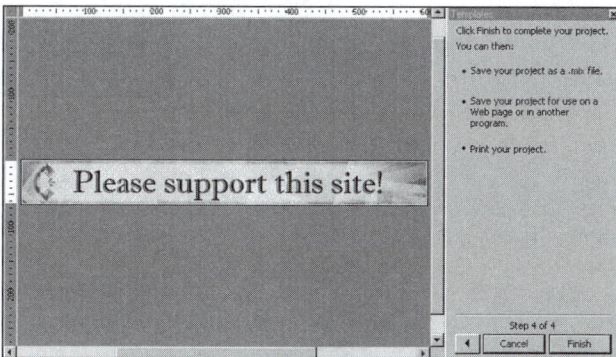

5.16

You can easily create all the graphics you need for a Web-site from the Web Graphics templates. Here is an example of how to create a Web banner. (See Chapter 13, "Creating Web Graphics," for more information about creating Web graphics.)

1. Choose a banner to customize by selecting File→New from Template and choosing Web Graphics from the drop-down list of templates. Double-click on the Site Banner category.

2. Double-click on a banner style to select it and to start the Template Wizard (5.15).

3. Click the Finish button to complete the design work (5.16).

(T) I P

Be sure to use a larger font size (24 points or larger) so that the text on the banner will be easy to read.

(N) O T E

To make a coordinating set of Web graphics quickly, choose the same style of graphic (Stone, Wood, HiTech, and so on) for each Web element you create.

Creating a Business Card from a Template

You can customize business cards by changing the font size and type, and by adding icons, logos, or clip art. Although there is no business-card template in PhotoDraw, you can create one in a few minutes by using a label template.

1. Select File→New from Template to open the Templates workpane. Select Business Graphics from the drop-down list of templates (5.17).

2. Select Labels–Address from the gallery of business graphic templates. The workspace behind the workpane fills with label styles.

3. Double-click on the label style you want to use for the business card (5.18).

4. Click the Next button to move to Step 3. Edit the text to remove the filler text and put in your business-card information (5.19).

5. Click the Next button to go to Step 4. Click the Finish button to end the use of the wizard.

(T) I P

Select the label that looks the most like a business card you'd like to use. Replace the picture during Step 2 of the wizard if needed by clicking the Browse button.

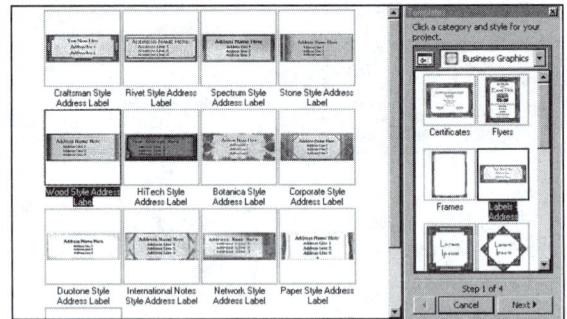

5.17

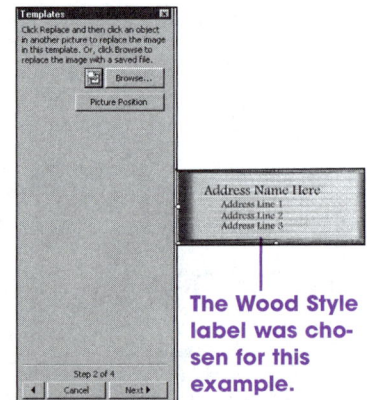

The Wood Style label was chosen for this example.

5.18

You must first delete the filler text on the template and then replace it with your text. Otherwise, editing text in a template is the same as editing text everywhere else in PhotoDraw.

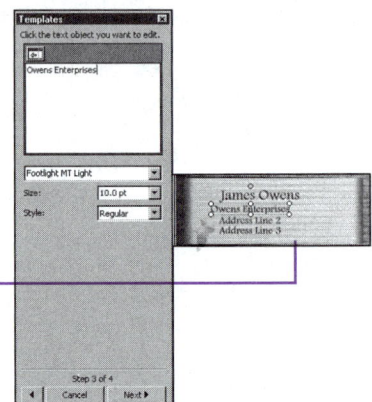

5.19

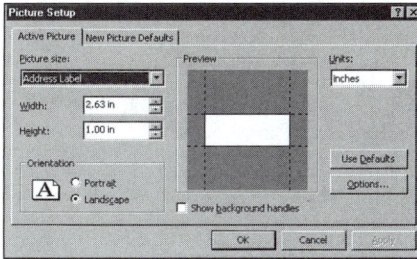

5.20

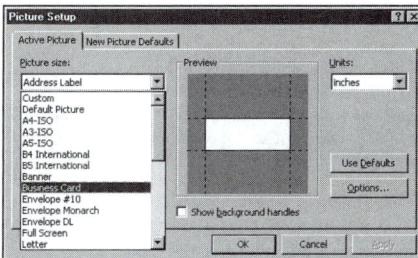

5.21

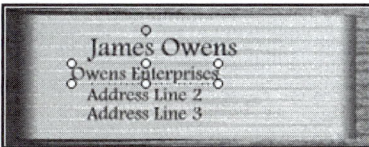

5.22

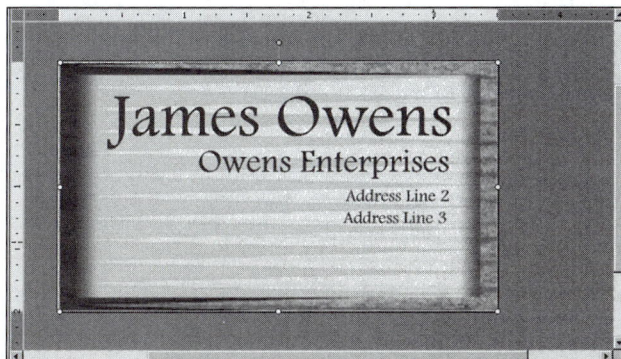

5.23

6. With the design still open and unsaved, select File→Picture Setup. The Picture Setup window opens **(5.20)**.

7. Click on the Active Picture tab and select Business Card from the drop-down list of picture size options **(5.21)**.

8. Click the OK button to use the new image size. PhotoDraw changes the size of the image background to business-card size **(5.22)**.

(N) O T E

You might have to rearrange or resize some of the elements on the design to make them fit the new size, but you won't have to make many changes. Select the object you want to resize, and use the selection handles to enlarge both the background and text elements **(5.23)**.

(N) O T E

Use the Print Reprints command to print multiple copies of your business card on business-card stock. See Chapter 15, "Printing Your Images," for more information on printing reprints.

Creating a PowerPoint Background from a Template

Although PowerPoint comes with its own ready-to-use templates, you can also use PhotoDraw to create PowerPoint templates. With PhotoDraw, you can customize every aspect of the background, including colors and images. After you've created one background, you can easily import it into PowerPoint and use it over and over again.

1. Open the Templates workpane by choosing File→New from Template. Select Business Graphics from the drop-down list of templates in the Templates workpane.

2. Scroll down to the bottom of the gallery of business graphics, and click on the PowerPoint Backgrounds icon. Templates of PowerPoint backgrounds appear behind the workpane (5.24).

3. Double-click on a background style to start the customization process. The workpane moves to Step 2 (5.25).

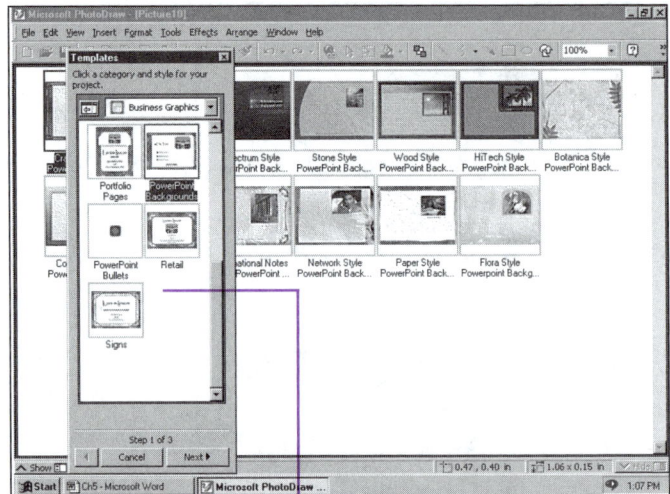

5.24

You can also create coordinating PowerPoint bullets using this same general procedure. Simply select the PowerPoint Bullets category on the Business Graphics category in the Templates workpane.

5.25

(T) I P

You can create customized text objects ahead of time and use them to replace pictures in template designs.

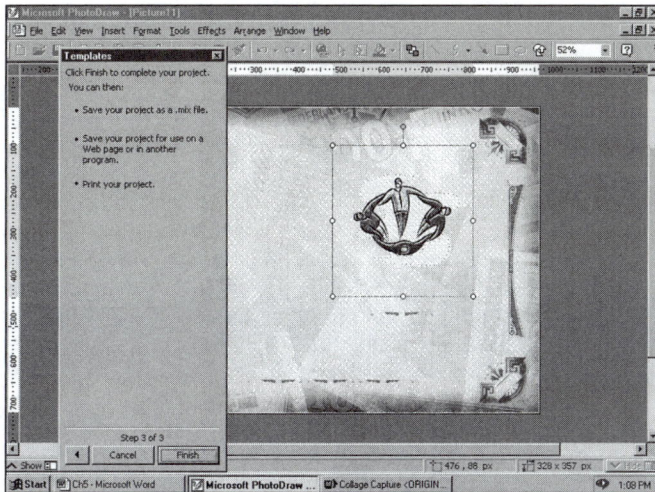

5.26   **After you have finished using the wizard, you can add text to the background as you would with any image.**

4. Replace the background picture with another one, if desired, by clicking the Browse button. Click the Next button to move to Step 3.

5. Click the Finish button to end the wizard **(5.26)**.

(N)OTE

You can create many customized elements using the templates, including icons and logos, and then combine them in other templates. Just follow the basic procedures outlined here.

(T)IP

Choose File→Save for Use In and select the As a Background for PowerPoint, FrontPage, or Word option. Walk through the wizard, and your final format will be a PNG file, something you can easily import into PowerPoint as a background.

(N)OTE

To use your finished background in PowerPoint, when you open PowerPoint, choose Format→Background. Click the down-arrow button under Background Fill, click Fill Effects, and then click the Picture tab. Click the Select Picture button and then select your PhotoDraw file.

CHAPTER 6

In this chapter you will learn how to...

Paint Lines and Effects

Change the Look of Brush Strokes

Create Special Effects Using Brush Strokes

Use Painting to Enhance Objects

Paint Frames for Objects

To create your own shapes and lines in PhotoDraw, you can either draw the elements or paint them. If you want a clearly defined, sharply detailed object, you'll want to use the draw tools. If you want to be more expressive, as you would be if you were using paints and a paintbrush, use the paint tools.

When creating shapes with the drawing tools, the Curve tool allows for interesting and surprisingly easy creation of shapes—it uses a

USING PAINTING TOOLS TO CREATE AND ENHANCE IMAGES

Bézier curve function that, once mastered in a short period of time, will enable you to create wonderful shapes. When you apply edges to the shape, especially photographic edges, you can create great-looking images—there are more than 150 photographic edges to chose from, making it easy to find an appropriate effect.

You can use the paint tools to perform simple painting effects, such as applying a color wash to an image. You can also use them to dramatically change the look of any object, including clip art and photographs. The more than 200 photo stamps open up fantastic new avenues for creative imagery—custom borders are now a snap. In this chapter, you'll learn the how the painting feature is used in PhotoDraw, how to change the appearance of the paintbrushes, and even how to do your own freehand painting. After you've learned those procedures, you'll be ready to use the more advanced painting effects, such as modifying and distorting parts of images by using brushes.

Painting Lines and Effects

If you want to loosen up and have a little more fun with lines in images, try using the painting tools to create your lines. You have many choices for styles and types of lines when using the painting tools, and you will find that even minor changes can make a great impact on an image or design when you're using this feature. Besides Plain, there are two other choices for brushes: Photo-Realistic and Artistic. Photo-realistic brushes are photographic images of objects that are suitable for painting and drawing lines, such as ropes, chains, and vines. Artistic brushes are brush strokes that look as though they had been painted with an artist's paintbrush.

1. Choose Tools→Paint Tools to open the Paint workpane (6.1).

2. Select a brush type by scrolling through the options shown in the gallery on the workpane. Click on one to select it (6.2).

6.1

Click on the Expand Gallery button to see all the brush styles at one time.

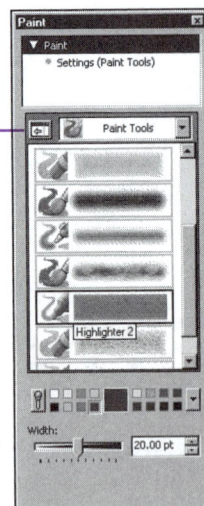

6.2

(T) I P

If you want a perfectly straight line, your best bet is to use the drawing tools to create one. Lines created with the painting tools aren't as crisp and clean as drawn lines.

(N) O T E

You can set the width of the line by moving the slider to the left or right or by typing a number in the Width box.

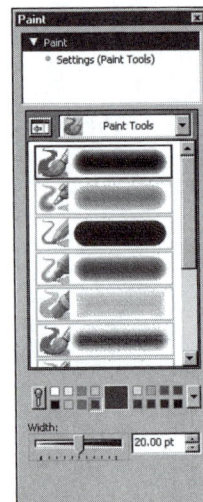

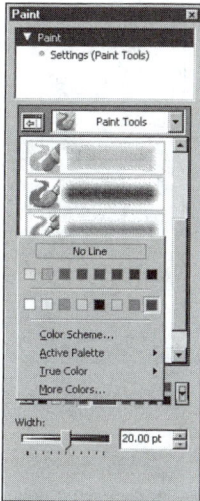

6.3

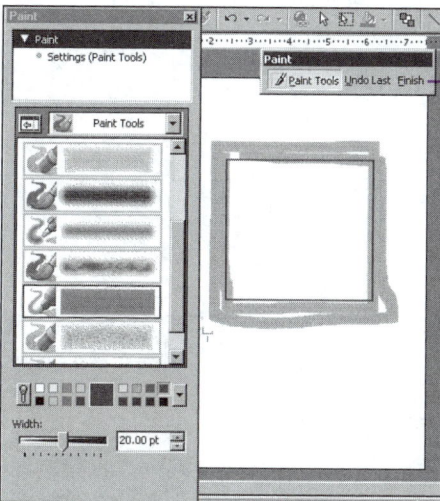

6.4

If you paint more than one line before clicking the Finish button, the lines are automatically grouped and can't be ungrouped.

3. Select a color for the brush stroke by clicking on one of the color squares or selecting a color from a palette seen below the gallery of line styles (6.3).

4. Click on Settings (at the top of the workpane) to change the transparency and width settings for the brush style you've selected.

5. Click on the document page to start painting. Hold the mouse button down while moving to the point where you want the line to end, and then release the mouse button (6.4).

6. Click the Finish button on the floating toolbar when you have finished your painting.

(T) I P

Create lighter-looking brush strokes by making the stroke more transparent. Making it thinner will also make the stroke look lighter.

(N) O T E

It's best to make your appearance changes and choices before you paint a line. You can't change them between the time you paint the line and the time you click the Finish button. After you click the Finish button, though, you can edit the line as you would any other PhotoDraw object.

Changing the Look of Brush Strokes

A painter or an artist rarely uses only one brush stroke to create a painting. She might use several brushes or use one brush in several ways to create myriad brush strokes. You can do the same thing with the painting brushes in PhotoDraw by combining and varying the brush settings while you are painting.

1. Select Tools→Paint Tools to open the Paint workpane (6.5).

2. Select the Chalk 2 brush (6.6) and adjust the settings so that you have a narrow (5 pt), transparent (50%) brush stroke.

3. Paint a few lines with this brush stroke.

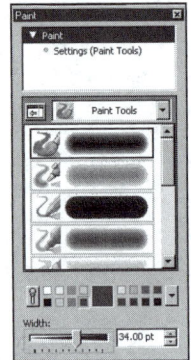

6.5

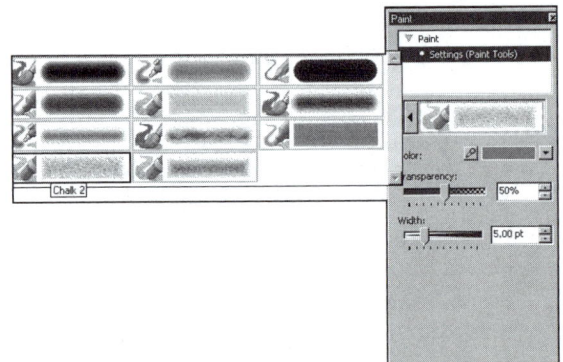

6.6

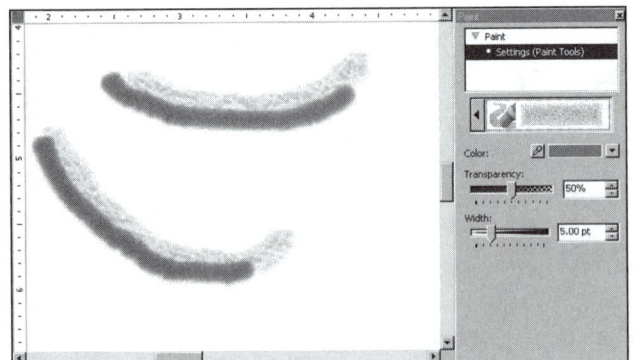

6.7

(T) I P

Make some lines shorter than others and keep layering lines and brush-stroke types (6.7), but don't use more than a few different types in one image.

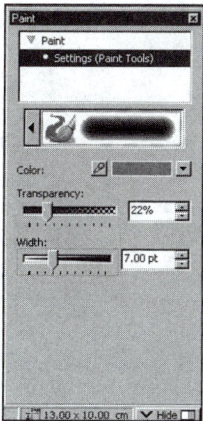

6.8

6.9

6.10

4. Increase the width and the transparency (6.8).

5. To increase the depth of the design, cover parts of a few lines you have already painted and then fill in any other blank areas.

6. Switch to a new color and repeat steps 3 through 7 until you are satisfied with the paint job (6.9).

7. Click Finish on the floating toolbar to end the painting process (6.10).

Ⓝ O T E

You can use the same basic procedure to draw with the photo-realistic or theme brushes, which you can access from the Edge workpane. Stick to one type of brush, and use various widths and degrees of transparency.

Creating Special Effects Using Brush Strokes

Although it's not painting in the normal use of the term, you can also use brushes to create special effects such as smudging and bulging areas of an image. These brush effects are useful for adding special effects to images and are especially effective with photographs.

6.11

1. Select the object you want to apply the special effect to **(6.11)**.

2. Select Format→Touchup and the pop-up list of touchup options appears **(6.12)**.

3. Select Smudge from the list of options. The Touchup work-pane appears with the Smudge Paint option selected.

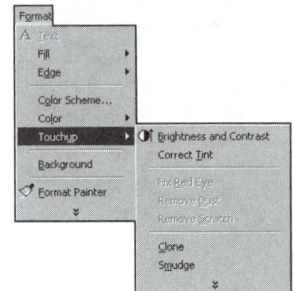

6.12

4. Click on the left-arrow key next to the brush to see the gallery of brush styles, and click on one to select it **(6.13)**.

To make a spiral smudge, paint a spiral shape with a wide brush setting.

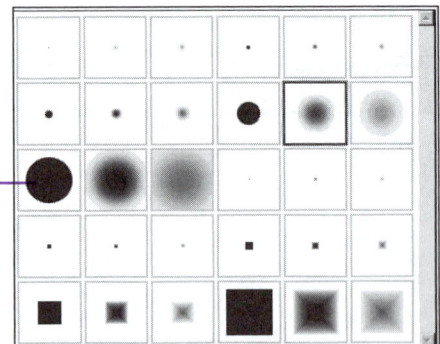

6.13

(T) I P

Take advantage of the different brush types to create different effects. For example, you can use the large brush sizes to make a wide effect or use the hard-edge brushes to create a sharper-edged smudge.

6.14

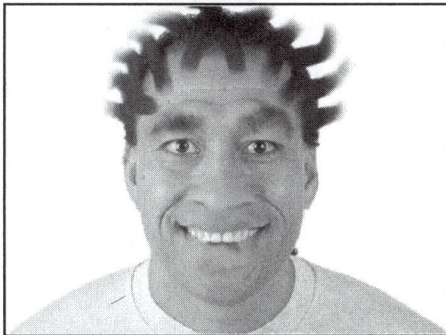

6.15

5. Set the degree of visibility and width of the smudge by moving the Amount slider.

6. Click on an area of the drawing you want to smudge, and drag to move the pointer to another area **(6.14)**.

7. Click the Finish button on the floating toolbar when you have finished your painting.

(N) O T E

You can use this same procedure to paint the object with other parts of the object (cloning) or erase portions of the object (erasing). Select the appropriate effect from the pop-up list on the Touchup workpane, and follow the steps listed previously.

(T) I P

The Smudge tool, when used in controlled ways, can be used to create comical effects **(6.15)** *when used on photos—if the photos are of friends and family, be sure they have a sense of humor first!*

Using Painting to Enhance Objects

You can use the painting effects in PhotoDraw to make almost any image look completely different. Here is an example of how you can enhance the appearance of a simple piece of clip art by using elements created with the artistic and photo-realistic brushes.

6.16

1. Open the image you want to enhance (6.16).

2. Select Tools→Paint Tools.

3. Select a brush type that is in keeping with the tone or message of the image, and set the width of the brush appropriate to the scale of the object. Typically, anything below 3 pt is too small to see.

6.17

4. Paint along some part of the object (6.17).

5. Switch to Draw Tools→ Scribble (6.18), and draw the lines you want to add to the image. It will add lines in the default color and size.

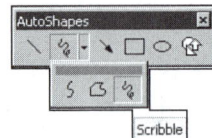

6.18

6.19

6.20

6. Shift+Click all the new lines you've created so each is selected.

7. Select a new color for the line from the current palette, or choose a new color from the drop-down color menu. You'll see all your selected lines change.

8. Select a width for the brush and an appropriate brush style **(6.19)**.

9. After you've decided the way you want your lines to look, you can select each one and reposition it based on the new width and style **(6.20)**.

(N) O T E

Select a simple line-art clip art image to practice your painting skills. A few quick painting effects make the image more useful and distinctive.

Creating Frames for Objects

Frames can help you draw attention to an image. They can also help you add visual interest to an otherwise boring image. You can draw a box around an image if you want to create a simple frame, or you can do something more creative. Either way you go, adding a frame in PhotoDraw takes no more than a few minutes, giving you plenty of time to experiment to find the frame you like the most.

1. Open the image you want to enhance (6.21).

2. Select Tools→ Draw Tools and choose the Scribble tool.

3. Draw a freehand border around the image (6.23).

4. With your frame selected, choose a point size for thickness, a color, and an artistic line type (6.24).

6.21

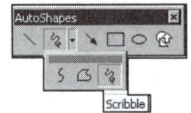

6.22

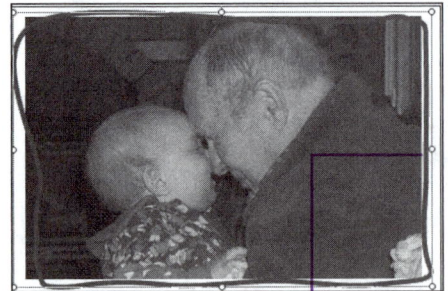

6.23 **The default line will normally be a 3 pt blue line until you change it to some other line type.**

6.24

6.25

6.26

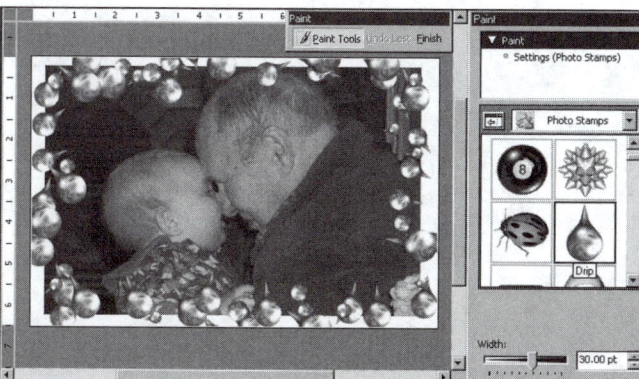

6.27

5. You can also choose a photo-realistic brush, which will give your frame a three-dimensional look **(6.25)**.

6. For a more subtle effect, you can adjust the transparency setting for your frame, allowing some of the orginal image edge to show through **(6.26)**.

(T) I P

For a really unique frame, consider using Photo Stamps. Tools→Photo Stamps will give you access to more than 200 images you can "spray" onto your image, and when used as a frame will give you interesting results **(6.27)**.

CHAPTER 7

In this chapter you will learn how to...

Draw a Line

Create a Curve

Draw with Autoshapes

Change the Shape of a Freeform Drawn Object

Attach Text to a Drawn Object

Add or Remove Arrowheads

Improve Objects with New Outlines and Fills

Design with Shapes

Create a Complex Design by Using a Few Basic Shapes

PhotoDraw offers two kinds of drawing tools: simple tools to draw lines, curves, and simple shapes such as circles and squares; and Autoshapes, predrawn shapes you select and then customize. Using the two sets of drawing tools together enables you to get the most work done in the least amount of time.

USING AUTOSHAPES TO CREATE AND ENHANCE IMAGES

The simple drawings of lines and basic geometric shapes is easily done by clicking and dragging. After you've created the basic drawings, you can easily change colors, shapes, sizes, and even the fill of the lines.

If you want to draw something more complex than a few lines or curves, you can use Autoshapes, the ready-to-use drawing shapes that can be created in a few seconds and then customized in various ways. The prepared shapes include lines, squares, stars, and banners. You can even draw flowchart shapes and callouts (message and thought balloons).

In this chapter, you'll learn how to draw basic shapes and use Autoshapes, and then you'll move on to learn about some simple and fast enhancements. You'll also walk through some examples of how to use drawing tools to create and improve images.

Drawing a Line

Frames and dividers, even the most complex and intricate ones, all start out as simple lines. PhotoDraw offers 20 basic line styles, so you have many choices.

1. Open the Edge workpane by choosing Tools→Draw Tools **(7.1)**.

2. Click the line icon on the Autoshapes floating toolbar. The cursor turns into a cross shape.

7.1

3. Scroll through the gallery of line styles, and click on one to select it **(7.2)**.

4. Make your color and width selections for the line by selecting a color and setting a width at the bottom of the workpane **(7.3)**.

You can apply a line style to a line after you've drawn it by clicking on the line and then clicking on a new style in the gallery.

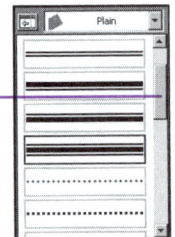

7.2

5. Click somewhere on the page to begin drawing. Hold down the left mouse button and drag the mouse to draw the line. Release the mouse button when you've finished drawing.

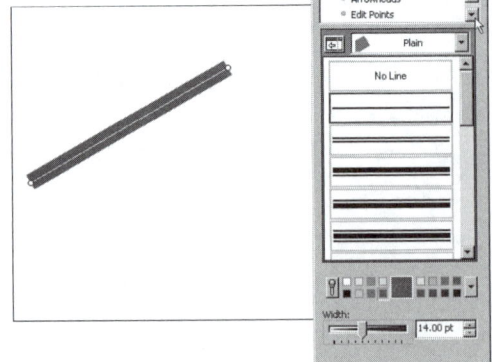

(T) I P

To draw a perfectly straight line, hold down the Shift key while drawing..

(N) O T E

You can draw a box or a circular shape by clicking on the rectangle or ellipse buttons on the Autoshape floating toolbar and following the steps outlined previously.

7.3

Creating a Curve

When you click on the Curve button, a down-arrow button appears. Click it to access the freeform and scribble Autoshapes if you want to use those types of curves.

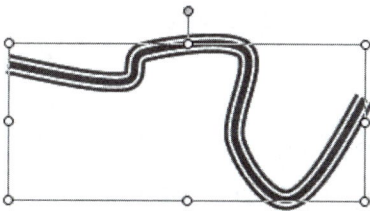

7.4

7.5

With the Autoshape curve, it's almost impossible to draw a curve badly. PhotoDraw gives you an incredible amount of control over what your curve looks like. Curves are useful for drawing things, of course, but with a little imagination you can find unexpected ways to use curved shapes.

1. Choose Tools→Draw Tools and the Edgework pane opens. Click on the Curve button on the Autoshapes floating tool-bar (7.4). The cursor turns into a cross shape.

2. Select your line style, colors, and widths from the workpane.

3. Click in the workspace to begin drawing. Holding down the left mouse button, drag the mouse and draw the line freeform (7.5). To draw a curve, you must click the left mouse button, which tells the pro-gram to anchor the curve there. Continue dragging and clicking as needed to draw the shape. Double-click the left mouse button to end drawing.

(T) I P

If your finished drawing will consist of the same few shapes used multiple times, remember that you can draw a few shapes and then copy and paste them. You don't have to draw each shape over and over again.

Drawing with Autoshapes

An Autoshape is the easiest way to draw anything more complex than a line or a simple geometric shape. This might seem confusing because the floating toolbar referred to in the preceding task is also titled Autoshapes, but this task refers to the predrawn geometric shapes provided inside PhotoDraw.

You can use one or more of the simple line-art shapes that come with PhotoDraw by selecting Shapes from the list in the Edge workpane.

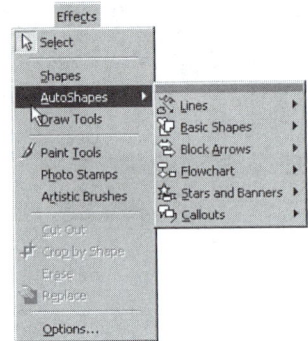

7.6

1. Select Tools→Autoshapes to open the pop-up list of shapes (7.6).

2. Click on one of the shape types to bring up the gallery of shapes. Select a shape by clicking on it (7.7).

3. Click in the workspace and, holding down the left mouse button, drag to create the shape (7.8).

4. If desired, change the look of the shape by making color, width, and line-style choices on the Edge workpane.

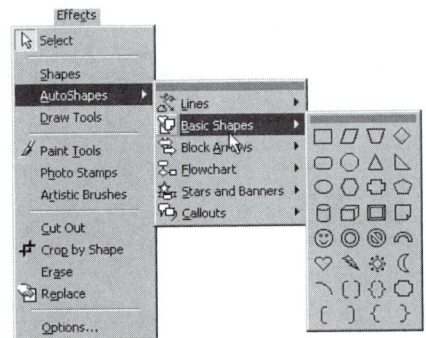

7.7

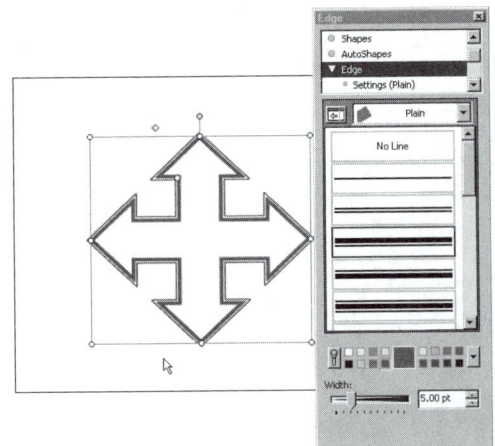

You can bring up a gallery of all the Autoshapes by clicking on Autoshapes in the list in the Edge workpane and selecting All from the pop-up list of Autoshape categories.

You might have to resize the object to reveal the shape you have chosen.

You can also bring up the categories of shapes by clicking on the Autoshapes icon at the top of the window.

7.8

Changing the Shape of a Freeform Drawn Object

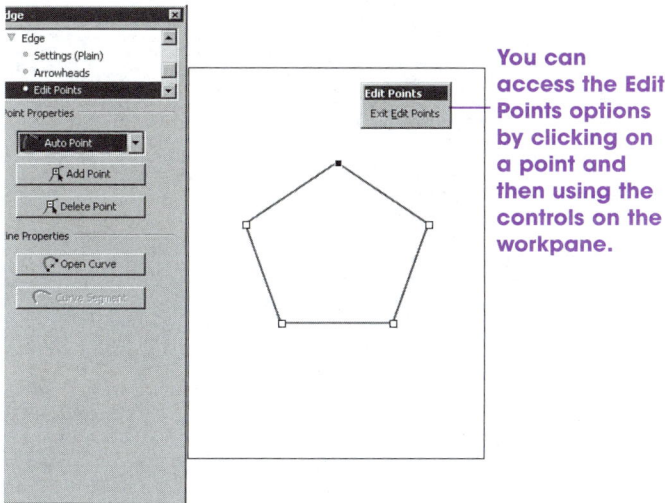

You can access the Edit Points options by clicking on a point and then using the controls on the workpane.

7.9

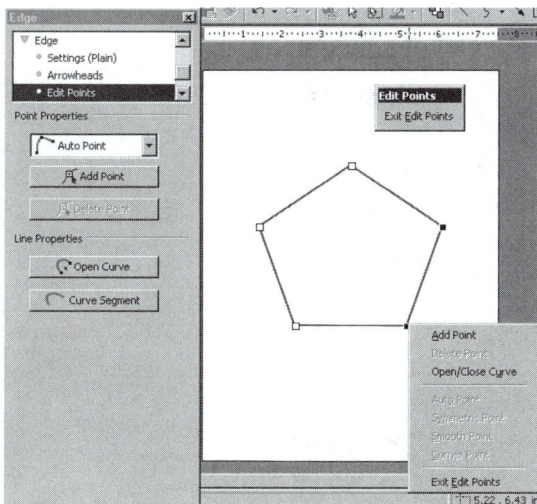

7.10

After you've drawn a shape using the freeform drawing tools, you can change the shape by tugging at the adjustment handles on the shape. Using these adjustment handles, you can completely reshape an image or just make minor adjustments.

1. Click on the object to select it.

2. Right-click the object and select Edit Points from the pop-up menu (7.9).

3. The Edge workpane appears with Edit Points selected. Edit points appear on the shape, and the workpane shows the point-editing options.

4. Right-click on a point where you want to reshape the object. The menu of options appears at the point (7.10).

continues

(N)OTE

To delete an edit point, select Delete Point from the pop-up menu that appears when you right-click on the point, or click the Delete Point button on the Edge workpane.

Changing the Shape of a Freeform Drawn Object continued

5. To add a point to the object, click on part of the drawing to select a segment, and then click Add Point **(7.11)**.

6. Click on an edit point and, holding down the left mouse button, drag the shape until you're satisfied with the change. To stop editing the shape, release the mouse button **(7.12)**.

7. When you have finished making all changes, click the Exit button on the Edit Points floating toolbar.

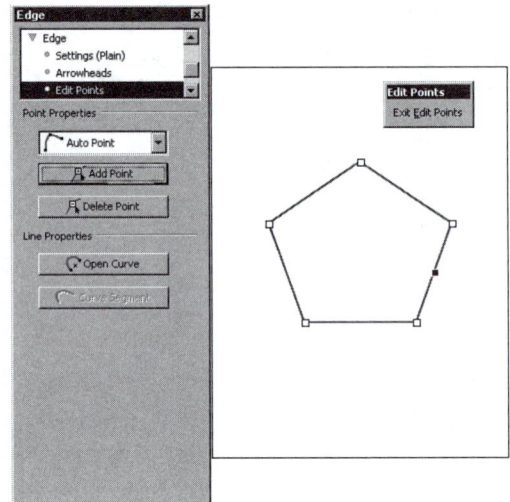

7.11

To delete a segment of the drawing, right-click on a point on the segment and select Delete Point.

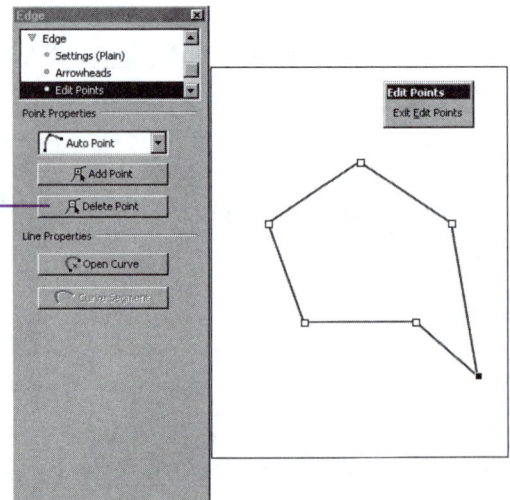

(T) I P

If you want to create a set of images that look alike (such as a set of Web graphics), try creating one shape first and then editing the points on several copies of the original image to make your set.

(N) O T E

You can change the shape of some Autoshapes by adding and deleting points. To find out whether you can do this, right-click on the object. If Edit Points appears on the pop-up menu, you can edit the drawing as described previously.

7.12

Attaching Text to a Drawn Object

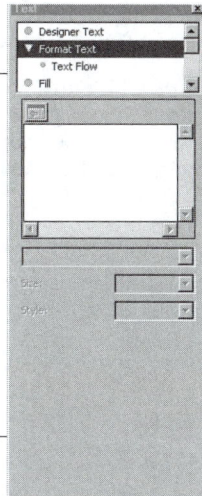

7.13

7.14

If you have created curved text in PhotoDraw, you might want to frame the text by using a single curve or a curved shape. Here's how you would create a curved shape and group it with the curved text. You can use this general procedure to group text with other shapes as well.

1. Open the file containing the curved text, and draw the desired curved shape **(7.13)**.

2. Align the text and shape by clicking on both and selecting Arrange→Align.

3. Select Arrange→Align→Align Center to align the text to the shape **(7.14)**.

4. If further adjustments are needed, click on the text or curved shape and move it.

5. Group the two objects by selecting Arrange→Group.

continues

(N) O T E

Use the alignment and ordering tools as needed to ensure that the text and drawn object line up the way you want them to.

Attaching Text to a Drawn Object continued

6. Repeat the entire procedure to add more text to the shape, if desired **(7.15)**.

After the two objects are joined together, you must ungroup them to edit the text.

7.15

7.16

(T) I P

After you have grouped your text and curve into one object, you can achieve some interesting effects by changing the shape of the grouped object **(7.16)**.

(T) I P

Be sure you click on all the objects you want to align before choosing Arrange→Align. Otherwise, you might have to go back and realign all the objects again because you left one out in the previous procedures.

(N) O T E

If you notice that after you've aligned objects, some part of an object is hidden by another, use the Order functions (Arrange→Order) to move the objects around until you can see all portions of the images that you want to see.

Adding or Removing Arrowheads

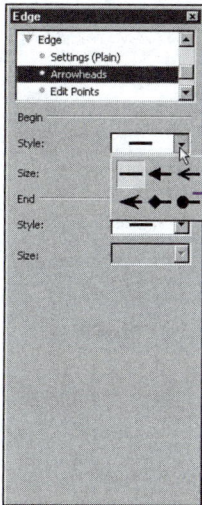

Adjust the size of the beginning or ending arrowhead by selecting a size from the pop-up gallery that appears when you click the down arrow next to the word Size in the workpane.

7.17

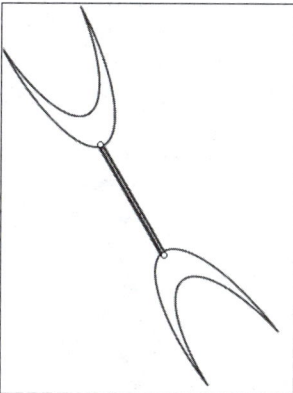

7.18

If you need to draw a plain arrow, try the arrow shapes in the Autoshapes collection before you try to draw your own. However, if you want a more distinctive look for your arrow, you can create your own by adding or removing arrowheads to a curved or straight line.

1. Draw the line in the workspace by opening the Outline workpane (Tools→Draw Tools) and drawing a line in the window.

2. Select Arrowheads from the list in the workpane. The arrowhead controls appear in the workpane.

3. If you want an arrowhead to appear where you began to draw the line, click the down arrow in the Begin section of the workpane, and select an arrowhead style from the gallery. To have the arrowhead appear at the end of the drawn line, select a style from the End section of the workpane (7.17).

(T) I P

Although you can add arrowheads to a line after you've drawn it, the easiest method is to have arrowheads selected when you first draw the line.

(N) O T E

If you don't like any of these arrowheads, you can draw your own and add them to the line by placing them at the beginning or end of the line and grouping the arrowheads and line together as shown in this fanciful example (7.18).

Improving Objects with New Outlines and Fills

You can easily change the color, width, and style of a line or shape by using the controls on the Edge workpane while you are creating the object. After you create it, you can change the look of the object even more by changing the fill inside the line.

Because a fill can be the most visually dominant portion of an image, changing a fill can really make a big difference in the appearance of an object. Try using contrasting lines and fills to change the look of an object quickly and easily. You will find more details on using Outlines and Fills to enhance images in Chapter 9.

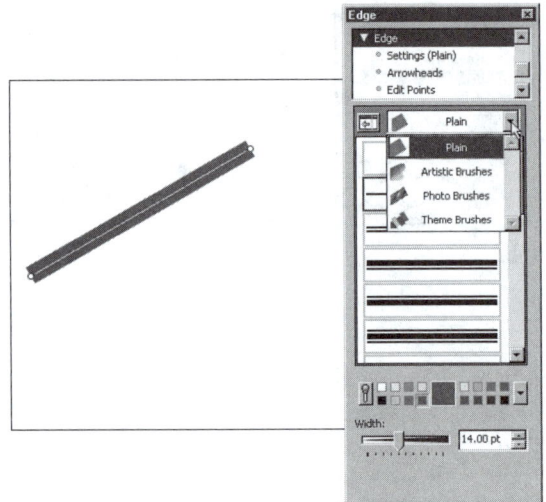

7.19

1. Click on the object to select it, and the Edge workpane appears (Tools→Draw Tools).

2. Click on the down arrow next to the word Plain on the workpane, and the drop-down menu of edge choices appears **(7.19)**.

3. Select the type of edge you want by clicking on one of the choices in the drop-down list. The appropriate gallery appears.

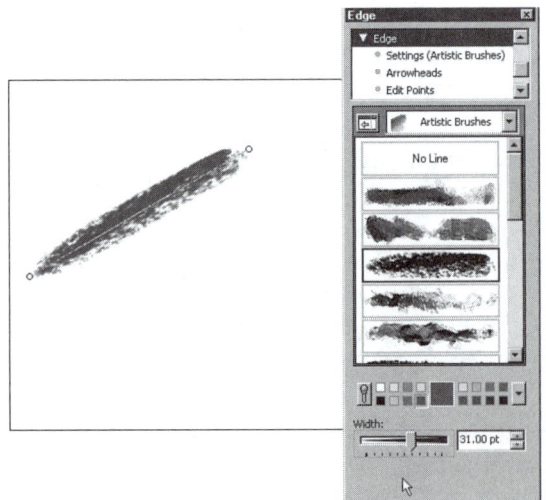

7.20

4. Scroll through the gallery and click on an edge style to choose it. PhotoDraw applies it to the image **(7.20)**.

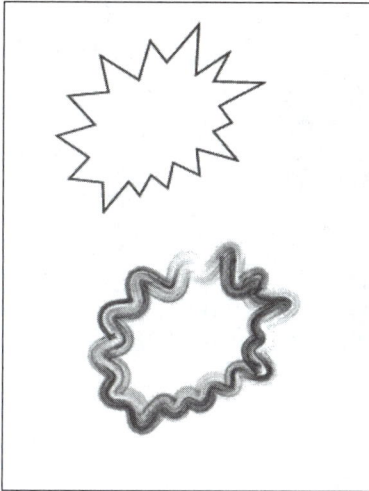

7.21

5. Make appearance changes such as width and color by using the controls on the work-pane as shown in this before-and-after example **(7.21)**.

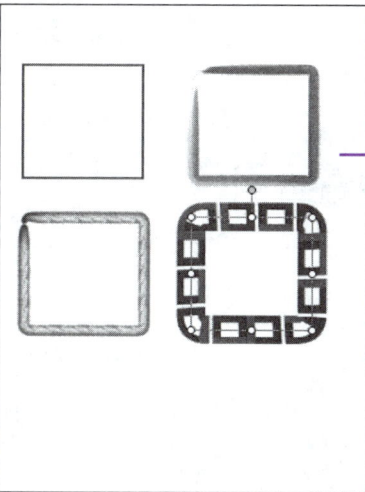

7.22

As shown in this fig-ure, even a simple shape like a square can look radically different when you change the style of the edge you're using.

(T) I P

If you want the neatness of drawing and the creative look of painting, you can get both by drawing a shape and then applying photore-alistic or artistic styles to the shape **(7.22)**.

(T) I P

You might have to widen the edge of an object when using the photorealistic or theme brushes in order to show all the detail in the edge you've chosen.

Designing with Shapes

You can create entire designs from shapes, or you can use shapes with other objects. You don't have to spend a lot of time designing with shapes, either; even adding one simple shape to an image can change the whole look. Here is a simple example of how you can change a photograph by using an Autoshape and some text.

1. Open the file containing the photograph to which you want to add a shape.

2. Select a shape from the Autoshapes gallery by selecting Tools→Autoshapes and choose a shape from the categories of shapes that appear on the menu **(7.23)**.

3. Draw that shape on top of the image you opened.

4. Resize and move the shape, if necessary, to make it blend in with the image **(7.24)**.

5. Add text inside the shape, if desired (Insert→Text), to create a completely new look for your photograph **(7.25)**.

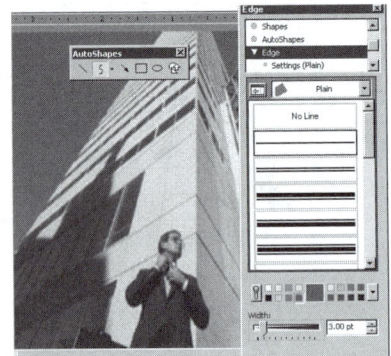

7.23

7.24

7.25

(T) I P

To make the shape stand out, you might have to fill the inside of the shape with light gray or white.

Creating a Complex Design by Using a Few Basic Shapes

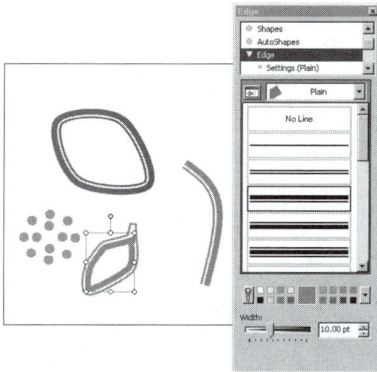

7.26

Don't worry if the drawn objects aren't perfect yet. You can always make appearance changes later as the design develops.

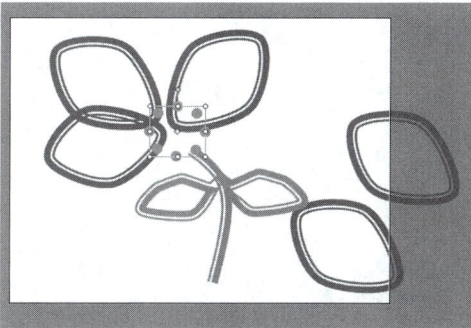

7.27

This process works best if you select objects that can be broken down visually into several smaller design elements.

7.28

You can draw a few simple shapes, and by copying, pasting, arranging, and resizing these elements, you can create a much more complex design. The results of such a process are limited only by your imagination because PhotoDraw takes care of the drawing capability! Here's an example of how to create such a design.

1. Draw the individual elements that will be used in the design by utilizing PhotoDraw's drawing tools (Tools→Draw) (7.26).

2. Copy and paste the objects you'll need more than one copy of.

3. Arrange the design by moving and rotating the objects as needed (7.27).

4. Continue moving and sizing objects as needed. Then layer them by using the Order command (Arrange→Order).

5. Change outlines or fills as needed to complete the design Format→Fill (7.28).

(T) I P

Group all the objects in the design before you save the design so that you can use the new drawing as a single object.

ⓒHAPTER 8

In this chapter you will learn how to...

Apply a Single Designer Effect

Apply Effects to Part of an Image

Modify Special Effects

Create an Antique Photographic Effect

Create a Sponge-Painting Effect

Create a Cartoon

Give Images a Hand-Drawn Look

Create a Watercolor Painting Effect

Modify Other Effects with the Texturizer Effect

The Designer Effects are some of the most powerful ways in PhotoDraw to transform the look of an image. Even simple black-and-white clip art can look like something you paid an illustrator lots of money to create.

Applying an effect takes no more than a few seconds, and there are literally hundreds of effects you can try. After you've learned to apply a single effect, you can go on and experiment with combined effects. After that, you can learn how changing the settings on effects changes the appearance.

USING DESIGNER EFFECTS TO ENHANCE IMAGES

The best part is that it takes only a few seconds to change effects and settings. That means you can experiment and follow your artistic intuition and impulses without taking a lot of time.

Using Designer Effects, you can make a bold image appear softer for use as a watermark or a background for a PowerPoint presentation with a few simple steps. PhotoDraw also enables you to modify certain Designer Effects by changing the settings or applying more than one effect to an image. There are countless uses for Designer Effects and as you become more proficient in its use, you will find that you can create professional-looking images in very little time.

In this chapter, you'll learn the basics of applying Designer Effects and then learn procedures for creating a few of the many effects that are possible. You'll also be presented with tips and tricks to make your own experiments much more profitable.

Applying a Single Designer Effect

Applying a single Designer Effect can change an entire image completely in a few seconds. You might find that you need to use only one carefully chosen effect to create an entirely new image from the basic one you started with.

Leave the setting on All to access the gallery containing all the types of Designer Effects.

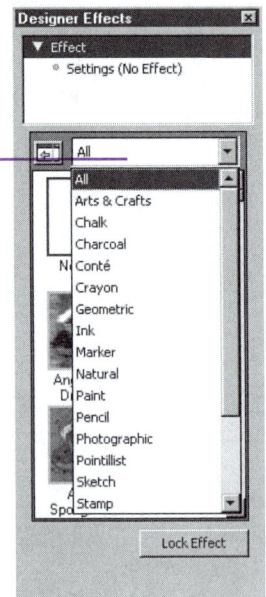

1. With an image open, select Effects→Designer Effects to open the Designer Effects workpane with the gallery of effects.

2. Select the type of effect you want to apply by choosing it from the drop-down menu of types **(8.1)**.

3. Scroll through the gallery and select an effect by clicking on the example tile. PhotoDraw applies the effect to your image **(8.2)**.

8.1

(T) I P

If you like a designer effect that is done in color, but you'd rather see it in grayscale, you can always apply the effect and then change the whole image to grayscale afterward (Format→Color→Grayscale).

(N) O T E

The procedures for applying any single Designer Effect to an image are the same for every effect. Just be sure to click the Lock Effects button when applying more than one effect to an image.

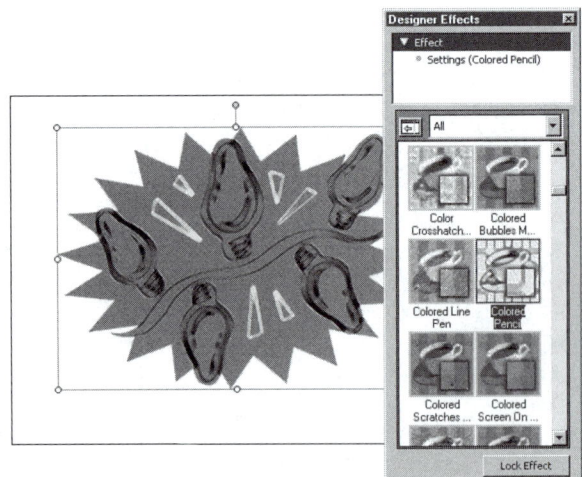

8.2

Applying Effects to Part of an Image

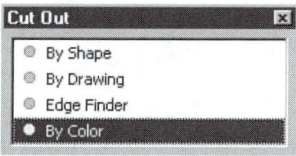

8.3

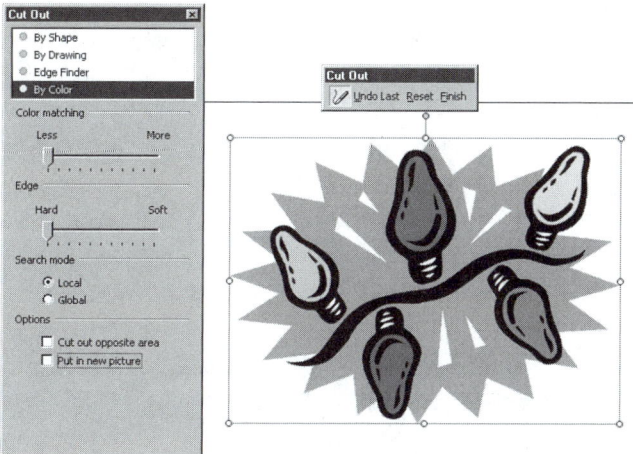

8.4

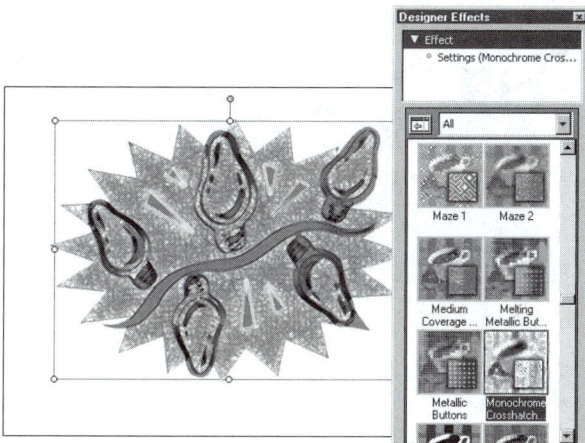

8.5

Always apply the effects immediately after you've selected the areas. If you close the image without applying the effects, the selection of the areas is lost.

A unique way to change an image is to apply these special effects to only part of an image. This process takes a little more time because you have to isolate the area from the rest of the image before applying the effect.

In this example, colors in the image are used to select areas in the image, a method that works well if the image has discrete color areas. You can use the other tools in the Cut Out workpane to select specific portions of other kinds of images.

1. Open the image and select Tools→Cut Out to open the Cut Out workpane.

2. Select By Color from the list of cutout options (8.3).

3. Select one or more areas in the image that are the same color.

4. Deselect the Put in New Picture option. Click the Finish button to select the areas (8.4).

5. Select Effects→Designer Effects to select and apply one or more Designer Effects to the selected areas (8.5). Click on the Lock Effect button after you have applied each effect if you want to apply multiple effects.

(N) O T E

You can also use the Crop tool (Tools→Crop by Shape) to isolate areas for applying special effects.

Modifying Special Effects

PhotoDraw gives you many choices for Designer Effects. You might never run out of effects to try, but just in case, you can also create many more effects by modifying any of the standard ones that come with PhotoDraw by changing its settings.

1. Click on an object to select it, and select Effects→Designer Effects to open the Designer Effects workpane.

2. Select the type of special effect you want to modify by selecting a type from the drop-down list on the workpane.

3. Click on Settings to bring up the appearance controls for that type of effect **(8.6)**.

(N)OTE

If the workpane for the special effect you choose has a brush setting, click the left-arrow key next to Brush to open the gallery of brush strokes. Click on a new brush stroke to use a different one. PhotoDraw changes the look of the image to reflect the change in the brush-stroke style **(8.7)**.

(T)IP

If you're going to experiment by applying several effects or making adjustments in several settings, duplicate the image first (Edit→Duplicate). That way, you'll always have the original image to compare to the edited one or to go back to if you don't like your changes.

Depending on the type of special effect you choose, there will be three or four special-effect controls you can use to change the look of the special effect. This effect has three controls.

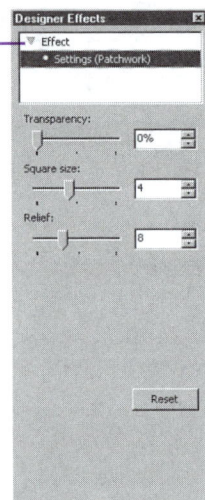

8.6

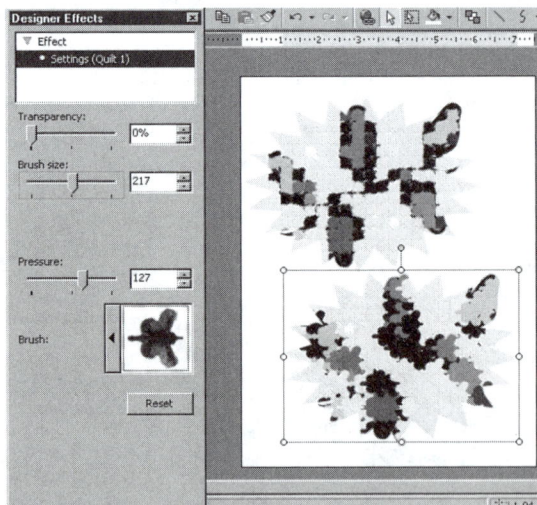

8.7

Creating an Antique Photographic Effect

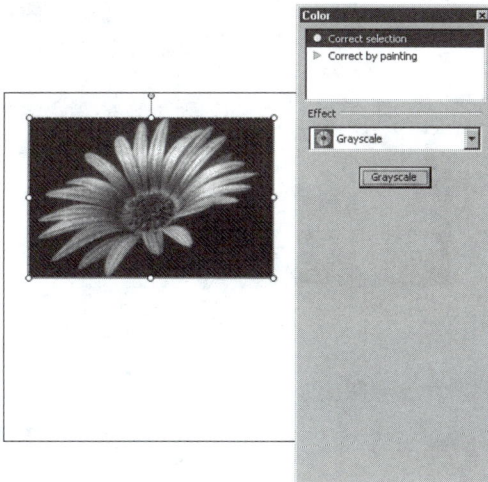

8.8

8.9 **To make the image look a little older, try combining the Film Grain and Grain effects, or the Film Grain and Diffuse Glow effects. You can also apply the Halftone Screen to the image if you want to turn it into a grayscale image like an old black-and-white photograph.**

Using various PhotoDraw editing tools, you can create a unique effect that results in an antique look for your photograph. This isn't a standard PhotoDraw-supplied effect, but rather one that I've developed and outlined in this task.

The antique photographic effect can be used on any image, but it looks more effective and authentic on photographs.

1. Open the image you want to alter, and select Format→ Color→Grayscale. The Color workpane opens (8.8). Click the Grayscale button to turn the image into a black-and-white one.

2. Select Effects→Designer Effects to open the Designer Effects workpane.

3. Select Photographic from the drop-down list of types of effects to open the gallery of photographic effects.

4. Select Film Grain by clicking on the sample image. PhotoDraw applies the effect to the image (8.9).

(T) I P *continues*

To add sepia tones to the image, choose Format→Color→Colorize and choose the RGB color from the More Colors→True Colors menu. Start with the settings Red 120, Green 80, and Blue 60, and experiment with the settings to get the tone you want.

Creating an Antique Photographic Effect continued

5. Click on Settings (Film Grain) in the list in the workpane, and the controls for the effect appear **(8.10)**.

6. Alter the four settings by using the sliders or typing numbers in the boxes until the image looks antique enough for your purposes **(8.11)**.

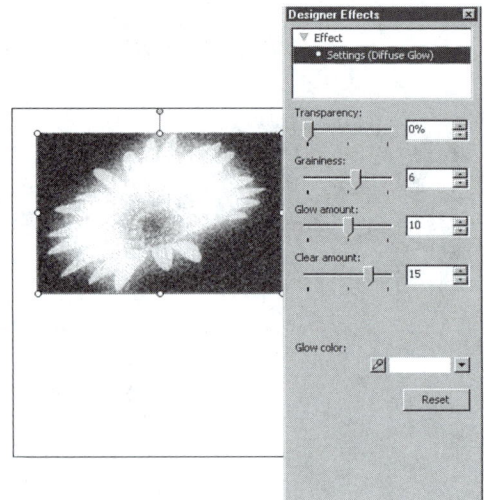

8.10

8.11

(N) O T E

If you are going to use a frame around the image, apply the frame before you apply the antique effects so that the look of the frame matches that of the image.

(T) I P

You'll have to experiment with all the settings on a particular effect to get the most out of the effect itself, so be prepared to spend a little time experimenting.

Creating a Sponge-Painting Effect

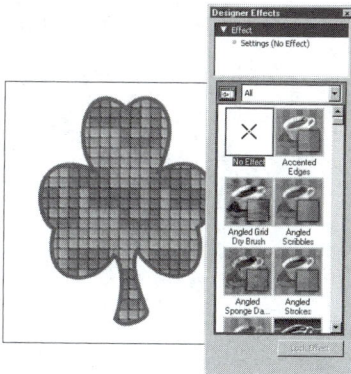

8.12

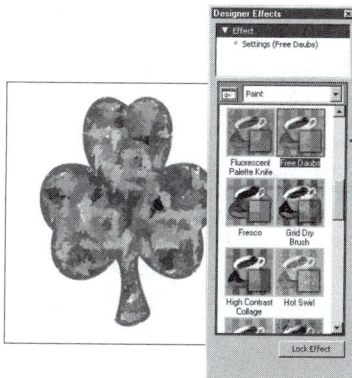

You could also use the Natural or Marker effects with the Sponge brushes to get a sponge-paint effect.

8.13

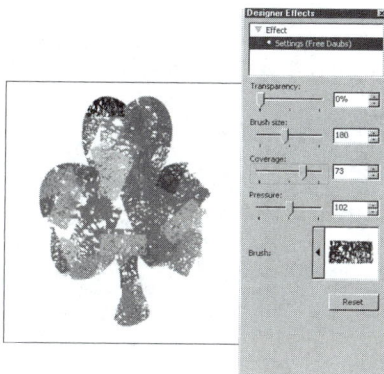

8.14

As you experiment with the Designer Effects, you will create your own ways to achieve a certain style or appearance as I have done. Here is one way to create a sponge-painting effect. After you've learned this one, experiment with a few of the other effects and their settings to create your own.

1. Open the image you want to change, and Effects→Designer Effects to open the Designer Effects workpane (8.12).

2. Select Paint from the drop-down list and select Free Daubs from the gallery (8.13).

3. Select Settings (Free Daubs) to access the controls. Change the brush to Sponge 1C (8.14).

4. After PhotoDraw has applied the change in brush stroke, you can further change the look by adjusting the settings on the workpane.

(T) I P

If you feel the paint effect you've applied gives too harsh a look to the image, change the transparency effect to 20% or 30% to soften the look.

Creating a Cartoon

Cartoons are a wonderful way to liven up many kinds of publications and presentations. With PhotoDraw, you can convert plain images into cartoonlike images with a few simple steps. This procedure turns an image into a black-and-white (or duochrome) cartoon drawing.

1. Select the image you want to change, and choose Effects→Designer Effects to open the Designer Effects workpane (8.15).

2. Select Sketch from the drop-down list of effects, and click on the Graphic Pen selection in the gallery. PhotoDraw applies this effect to your image (8.16).

3. Click on Settings (Graphic Pen) and change the stroke direction to Vertical.

4. After you change the stroke direction, PhotoDraw applies the change (8.17).

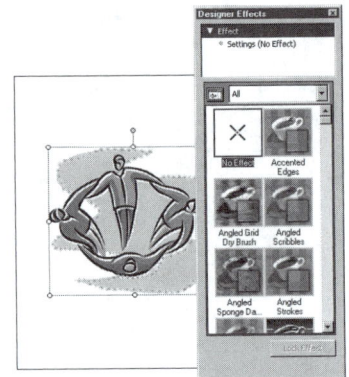

8.15

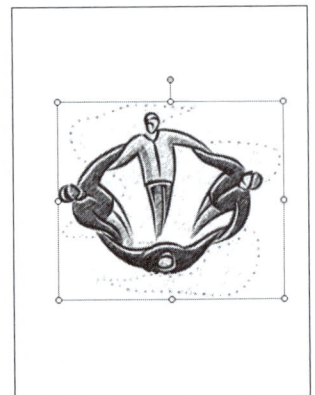

8.16

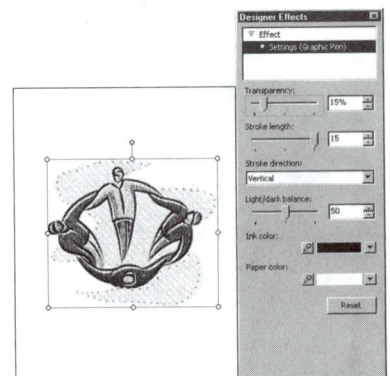

8.17

Ⓝ O T E

You can change the color of the strokes and the color of the background by selecting new colors on the Settings workpane.

Ⓣ I P

If you have a colored image and want some of the color to show after you've applied the effect, change the transparency to something higher than 0%.

Giving Images a Hand-Drawn Look

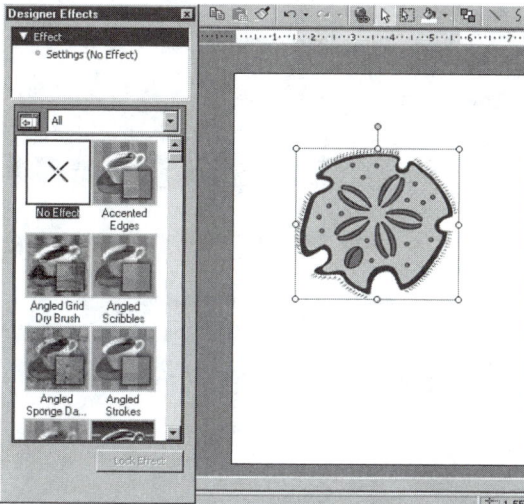

8.18

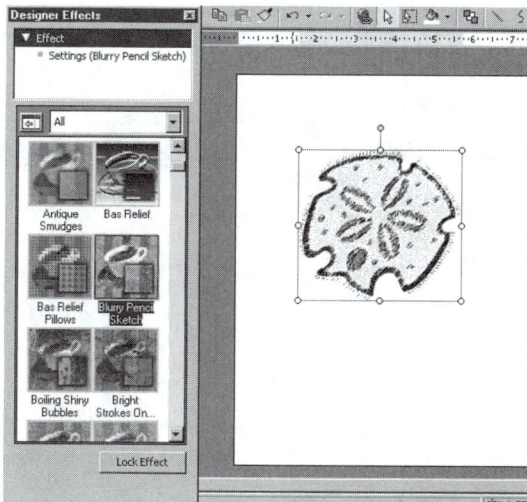

8.19

People use pencils, pens, charcoals, and lots of other materials to draw images. PhotoDraw has Designer Effects brushes that simulate all of these looks, so you can choose your drawing style after you've applied an effect. Here is one way to apply a delicate pencil-drawn look to an image.

1. Open the image you want to change, and open the Designer Effects workpane by selecting Effects→Designer Effects (8.18).

2. Select Pencil from the drop-down list of effect types, and select Blurry Pencil Sketch in the gallery (8.19).

3. Click on Settings (Blurry Pencil Sketch) and select Pencil3C. The name of the brush settings pops up when your cursor passes over the example.

4. Change the Transparency setting to 25% and the Brush Size to 75.

continues

(N) O T E

Don't forget to click the Lock Effect button when you have finished making changes to the image or when you are applying more than one effect to the same image.

Giving Images a Hand-Drawn Look continued

5. PhotoDraw applies the new settings **(8.20)**. You can further change the look of the image by adjusting the other settings **(8.21)**.

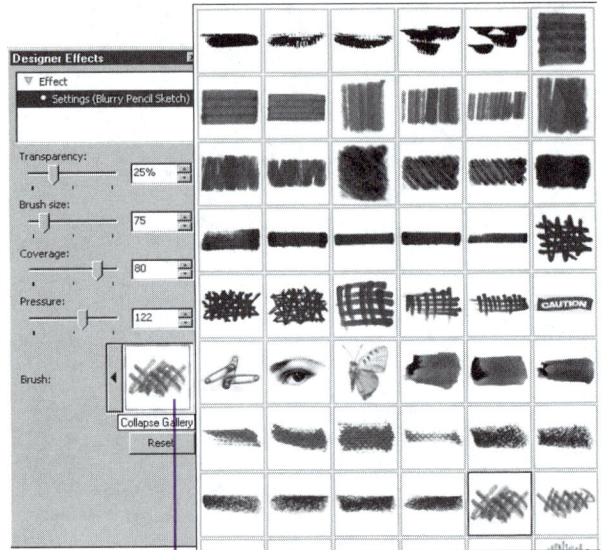

8.20   **Experiment with pencil settings and brush sizes to vary the look of the image even more.**

Some of the details of the effects you will achieve with the painting Designer Effects will not be noticeable if you are not able to print the final result in color. If you're going to print your image in grayscale, make the image grayscale first and then add Designer Effects so you can create details that will be seen later.

Because there are so many possibilities with Designer Effects and you can't save any of the combinations you create, be sure to take detailed notes each step along the way so you can re-create the same cumulative effect on other images later.

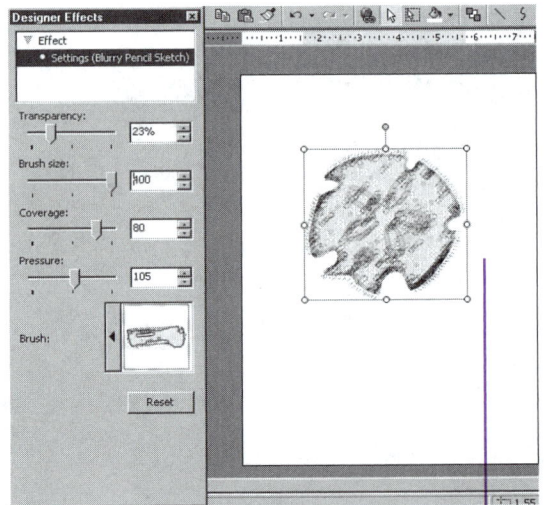

8.21   **Changing the type of brush, the brush size, and pressure will make the most visible differences in your image. In this example, the brush was made much larger with a setting of 400.**

Creating a Watercolor Painting Effect

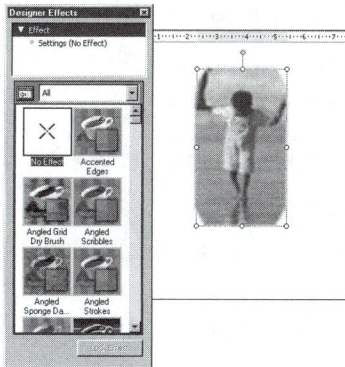

8.22

8.23

8.24

Not many of us are grand master painters, but we all like the looks of a beautiful oil or watercolor painting. With the Designer Effects in PhotoDraw, even the simplest clip-art images can take on a look of classic elegance with the painting effects.

1. Select the image you want to use, and choose Effects→ Designer Effects to open the Designer Effects workpane (8.22).

2. Select Arts and Crafts from the list of effect types, and then select Poster Edges from the gallery. Click the Lock Effect button to lock the effect (8.23).

3. Select Paint from the list of effect types and then Water-color from the gallery to complete the transformation (8.24).

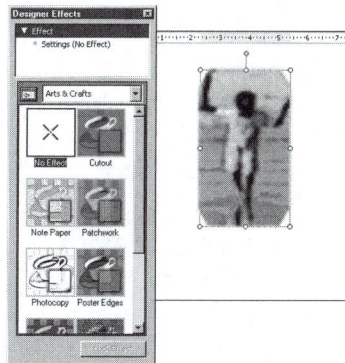

You don't have to use this step to apply a watercolor look, but doing so helps retain the details in the image after you apply the watercolor effect.

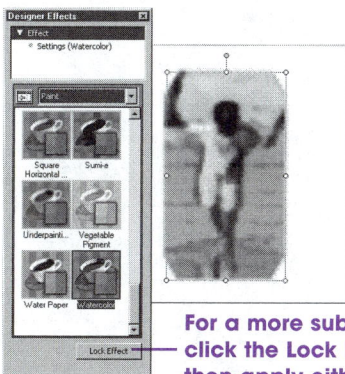

For a more subtle watercolor effect, click the Lock Effect button and then apply either the Underpainting or Water Paper effect after you apply the Watercolor effect.

(N) O T E

An easy way to apply an oil-painting effect to an image is to apply the Fingerpaint effect and then change the brush to one of the Paint brushes.

Modifying Other Effects with the Texturizer Effect

The Texture settings enable you to alter an image so that it looks as though it were printed or painted on a particular kind of surface, such as canvas or burlap. You can apply the Texturizer effect alone or in combination with other effects. Here's an example of how to use it along with another type of effect to get the effect of an embossed image printed on fine paper.

8.25

1. Select the image to use, and then choose Effects→Designer Effects to open the Designer Effects workpane (8.25).

2. Select Surface from the list of effect types and then Bas Relief from the gallery to obtain an embossed effect in black and white (8.26).

   If the Bas Relief setting doesn't give you the embossed look you want, try the Emboss or Chrome effects.

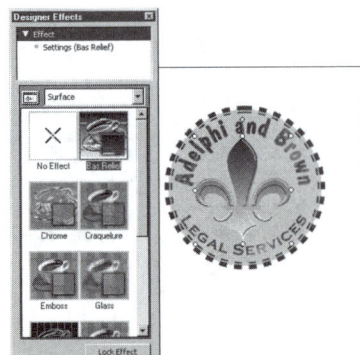

8.26

3. Click the Lock Effect button before proceeding.

4. Select Texture from the drop-down list of effect types and then Texturizer from the effects gallery (8.27).

   PhotoDraw applies the effect using the surface type that was used last. You will have to open the gallery of types to apply any other surface types.

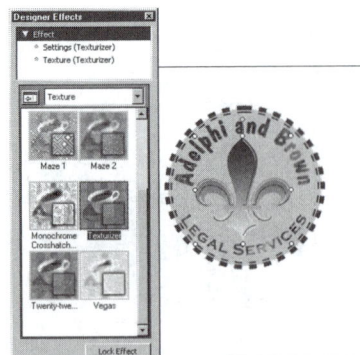

8.27

(T) I P

Try changing the fill on a simple object to something with more apparent detail before you apply the Bas Relief effect. The Bas Relief effect will be more apparent if you do.

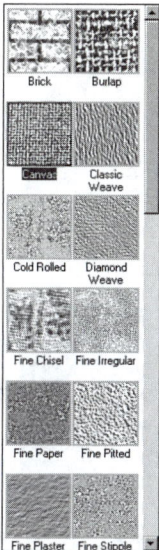

8.28

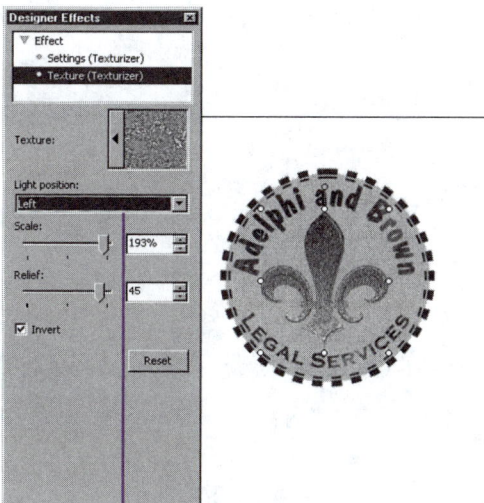

8.29   **To change the look of the highlights and shadows in the texture, change the Light Position setting.**

5. Click on Texture (Texturizer) and the workpane changes to show the Texturizer controls. Click on the Texture left-arrow key to show the gallery of texture types (8.28).

6. Click on Fine Paper in that gallery and alter the texture controls as necessary to get the look you want (8.29).

ⓃOTE

If you like the basic shape of any object, but don't like the details or the fill, using Designer Effects is a good way to use the shape and get rid of the details entirely. Designer Effects can also be used to create a series of images with the same shape but with entirely different looks—a good idea if you want to coordinate Web site material with a slideshow presentation.

CHAPTER 9

In this chapter you will learn how to...

Change the Fill of an Image

Fill an Image with a Picture

Apply an Edge to an Object

Select an Edge Type

Soften the Outline of an Image by Using Edges

Frame Images with Designer Edges

Create a Filled Frame

Use Edges and Fills to Enhance Clip Art

The use of fills and edges to change the appearance of text objects is covered in Chapter 3. In this chapter, we explore the use of fills and edges to change the appearance of nontext objects.

There is almost no end to the kinds of fills you can use or create with PhotoDraw. Solid colors, textures, two kinds of gradients, and even photographs are all fill types you can use.

USING THE FILL AND EDGE TOOLS TO CHANGE IMAGES

The procedure for changing fill types is the same for all types, so after you've learned how to change one type of fill, you can use the same basic procedure to change other types.

Edges in PhotoDraw are more than simple lines, although simple line edges are possible. You can also use edges to outline objects by using artistic lines that look as though they were hand-painted or lines drawn in photographic images.

In this chapter, you'll learn how to change the fill in an image, including how to fill an object with a picture. You'll also learn how to apply an edge to an object and how to change the appearance of edges. You'll see an example of how using a fill change and an edge can dramatically change the look of an ordinary object.

Changing the Fill of an Image

The fill in an image or a portion of an image contributes significantly to the appearance of the image. Changing or adding a fill can make the image look completely different.

1. Select Format→Fill→Solid Color and the Fill workpane appears (9.1).

2. Select a color for the fill by clicking on one of the small squares of color (9.2). This is the basic procedure for applying fills to images.

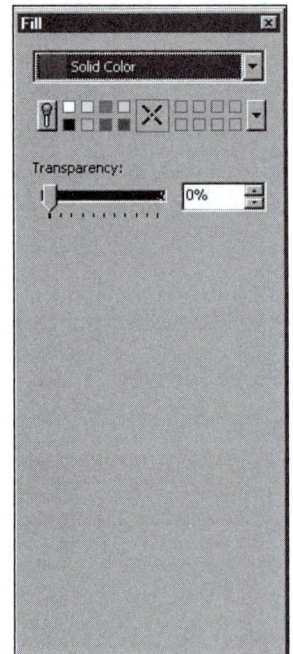

9.1

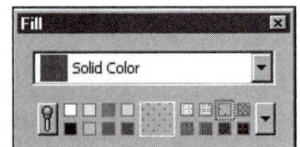

9.2

(N) O T E

Adjust the transparency of the color fill by moving the Transparency slider or entering a number in the Transparency box.

(N) O T E

PhotoDraw fills the entire image with the fill you select unless you first select a portion of the image to be filled by using the Cut Out or Crop tools.

Filling an Image with a Picture

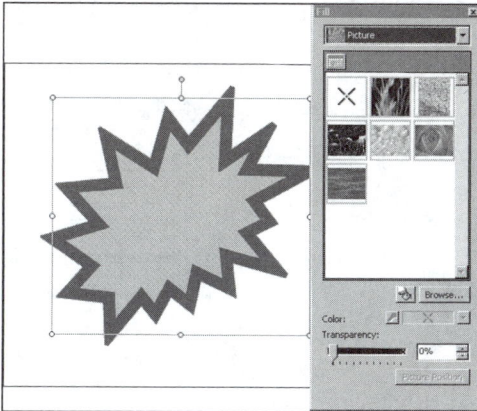

9.3

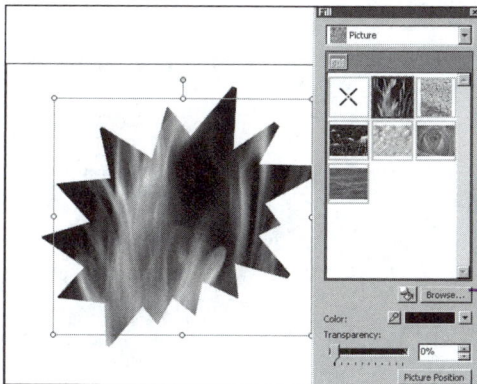

If you want to use an image that is not in the gallery, click the Browse button and locate the desired file.

9.4

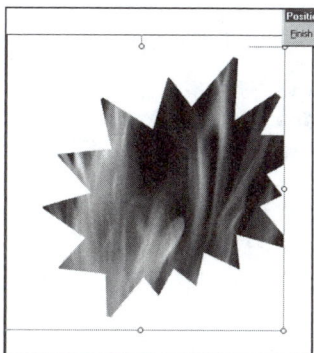

Click the Finish button when you are satisfied with the position of the picture within the shape.

9.5

PhotoDraw allows you to fill any object with a picture and to adjust the picture to allow specific details in the picture to appear. After you have filled the object with a picture, you can use any of the photographic editing tools in PhotoDraw to continue to alter the appearance of the image.

1. With an image open that you want to fill, select Format→Fill→Picture to open the Fill workpane **(9.3)**.

2. Click on one of the pictures in the gallery to use as your fill **(9.4)**.

3. If you want to select a picture from another file, click the Replace button and then the Browse button to open the file directory. When you've located the file you want to use, click on the name of that file.

4. To alter the position of the picture that fills the shape, click the Picture Position button on the Fill workpane. Click on the picture in the area to select it, and drag the mouse to move the picture around **(9.5)**.

(T) I P

To create a custom photographic outline for an object, copy the object and fill it with another picture. Then enlarge the copy slightly and place it behind the original.

Applying an Edge to an Object

You can surround the outside of an object or part of an object with an edge in PhotoDraw. Doing so helps accentuate the shape of the object or draw attention to the object. In addition, by changing the size, color, or style of an edge, you can make your object more appealing and creative.

1. Select the object or portion of the object you want to edge, and select Format→Edge to open the list of edge options.

2. Select an edge type from the drop-down list, and the Edge workpane opens, showing the gallery of edging styles **(9.6)**.

3. Scroll through the gallery of edge styles, and click on one to select it. PhotoDraw applies the edge to the object **(9.7)**.

4. To change the color of the edge, click on one of the color squares or click on the down arrow to access the other color palettes.

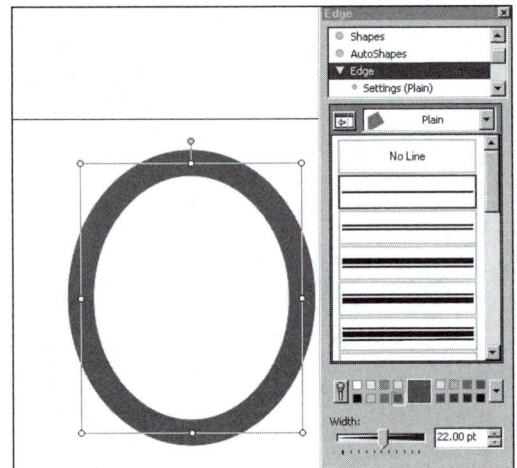

9.6

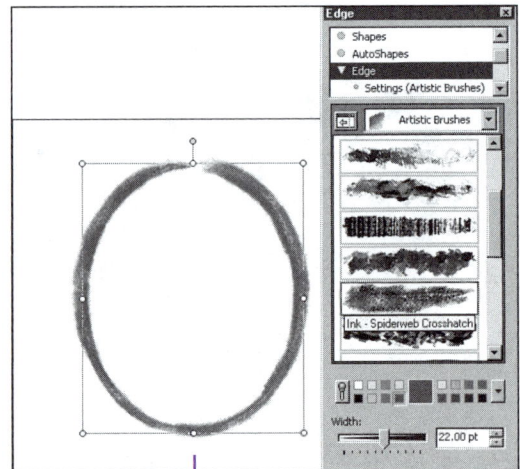

9.7 **The Artistic edge was chosen for this example, but the same basic procedure works for all edge types.**

(T) I P

To create an edge that coordinates with the colors in the image, use the Eyedropper tool to select a color from the image.

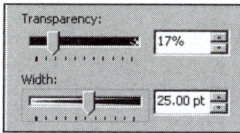

9.8

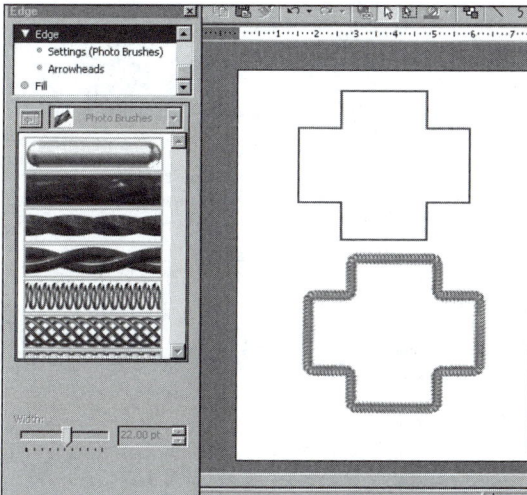

9.9

5. To further change the appearance of the edge, select Settings from the list in the workpane. Use the sliders or windows to change the transparency and width of the edge **(9.8)**.

(T) I P

*Adding a distinctive edge to an object can make even a very simple object such as this one stand out and be more noticeable **(9.9)**.*

Selecting an Edge Type

You can choose the edge type (Plain, Artistic, Theme, or Photo) before you choose an edge style, or you can change to another type after you've applied an edge. If you know what kind of edge you want to use, choose it before you apply it. If you want to experiment with the look of the edge, change the style after you've applied it.

1. After you have applied the edge, click the down-arrow key in the workpane to open the list of edge types (9.10).

2. Click on one of the types to open the gallery of edge styles for that type.

3. Click on one of the edge styles in the gallery to apply it (9.11).

4. To change the settings for the edge type, click on Settings on the workpane list, and use the sliders or enter a number in the boxes to make adjustments as needed.

(T) I P

Use plain edges to draw subtle attention to what's inside the edge (9.12). Use the artistic and photo edges when you want to add artistic flair to an image.

(N) O T E

To select the edge type before you apply an edge, select the type from the pop-up menu that appears when you select Format→Edge.

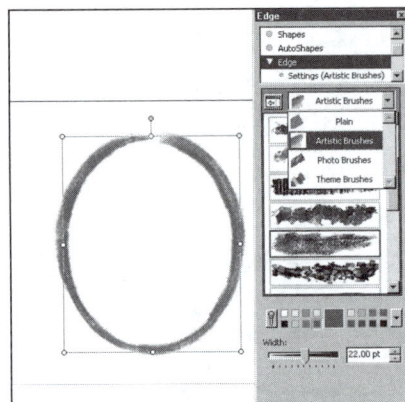

9.10

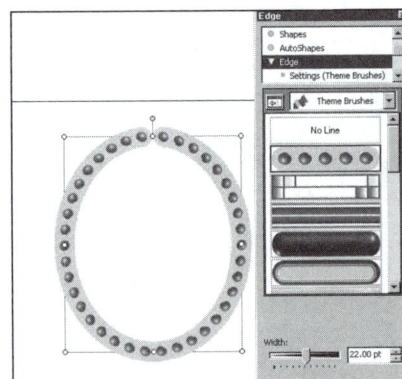

9.11

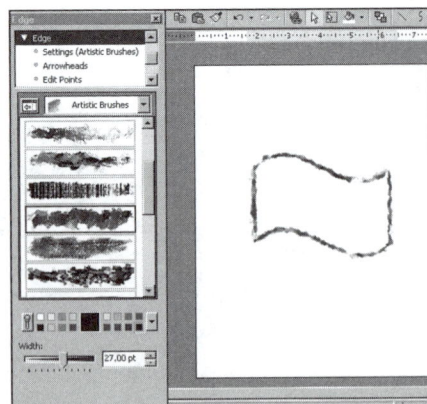

9.12

Softening the Outline of an Image by Using Edges

9.13

9.14

9.15

In this image, one basic shape (the flower) was copied, pasted, and resized several times. Then each flower was softened a different amount and arranged. One flower was even placed on the vase to look like a stencil.

If you want to make the edges of an object look softer or slightly out of focus, you can soften edges of an object or a portion of the object. Being able to do this comes in handy when you want a softer look to an entire image. It also helps to make for a more natural-looking merge if you are placing the object in another image.

1. Open the image you want to apply this effect to, or select a portion of an image (9.13). Select Format→Edge→Soft Edges to open the Soft Edges workpane.

2. Change the slider setting to something higher than 0 to soften the edges (9.14).

(T) I P

You can create a very interesting image by copying and pasting, and then arranging the copies artistically (9.15). Finally, give depth to the new image by softening the edges of each copy a different amount.

(N) O T E

Softening the edges applies a blurry effect to all edges of the object. The higher the setting, the lighter the entire image appears.

Framing Images with Designer Edges

Another type of edges in PhotoDraw, called Designer Edges, allows you to apply Artistic, Paper, and Traditional edge looks to all four sides of an image at one time. In other words, you can use this edge type to frame the image or a portion of the image. You can use Designer Edges to apply a simple frame, or you can be more creative with the effect. For example, you could create a strip that looks as though it were torn from a sheet of paper to use on a Web page or in a PowerPoint presentation.

1. Click on the object or the image you want to apply the effect to (9.16).

2. Select Format→Edges→ Designer Edges to open the Designer Edges workpane (9.17).

3. Click on the down arrow next to the word Artistic to access the list of Designer Edge types.

4. Click on one of the examples of edges in the gallery that appears. PhotoDraw applies the effect to the image (9.18).

9.16

9.17

Ⓝ **O T E**

If you want to move the position of the picture within the Designer Edge frame you've created, click the Picture Position button on the workpane and click on the picture to move it around.

Click the Stretch to Fit button to apply the effect to the entire image or object.

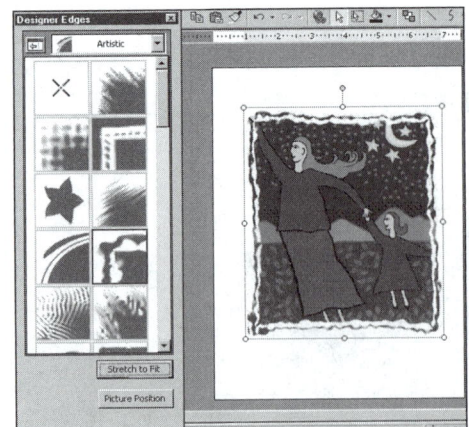

9.18

Creating a Filled Frame

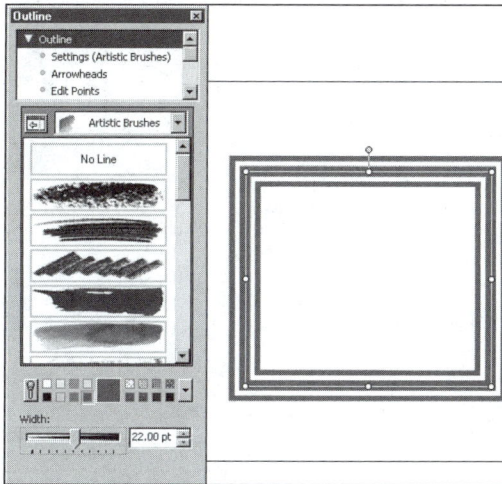

9.19

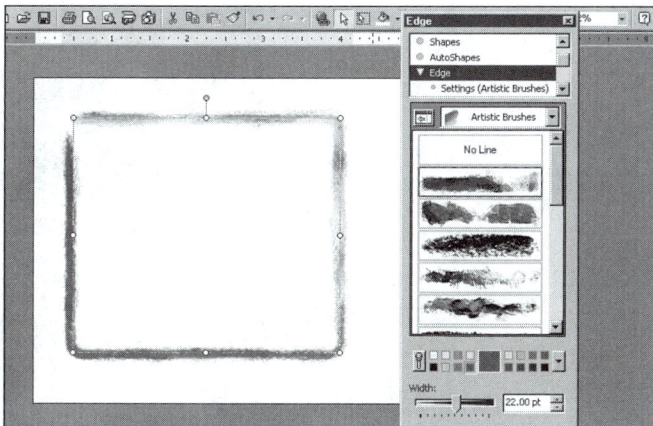

9.20

By combining the edge and the fill effects, you can coordinate the two in one new image. How different the new image will look depends on your fill and edge choices. To demonstrate this point, here is an example of creating a square that looks as though you drew it by hand.

1. Use Tools→Draw Tools to open the Edge workpane. Click on the Square icon on the floating toolbar, and select the Thin-Thick-Thin line type and draw a square. **(9.19)**.

2. Select the Chalk Loose Sketch artistic brush from the Artistic Brushes gallery **(9.20)**.

3. Select Settings (Artistic Brushes) from the workpane list, and change the amount of transparency to 50% and the width to 25 points.

continues

(T) I P

When you draw a frame around around an object, make the frame width wide enough so that the frame is noticeable, but not so wide it overpowers the image inside the frame.

Creating a Filled Frame continued

4. Be sure your object is selected, and select Format→Fill→ Picture to open the Fill work-pane and gallery of picture fills.

5. Select the Cloudy Sky fill by clicking on the thumbnail example. Change the trans-parency setting to 50% **(9.21)**.

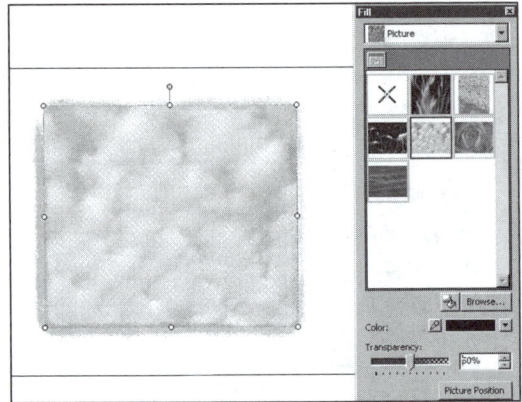

9.21

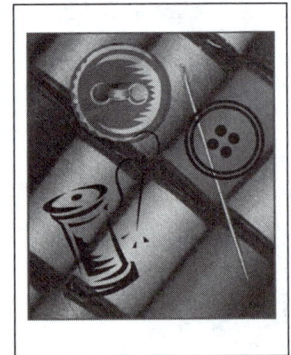

9.22

(N)OTE

You can create interesting collages by filling a large square with a photographic image and then cropping images of related items and placing them within the large square **(9.22)**.

(T)IP

Another way to change the appearance of an object by using this procedure is to set the transparency of the edge at 75% and the transparency of the fill at a different setting, such as 50% **(9.23)**.

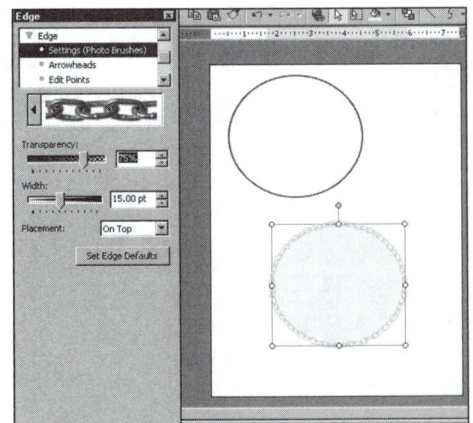

9.23

Using Edges and Fills to Enhance Clip Art

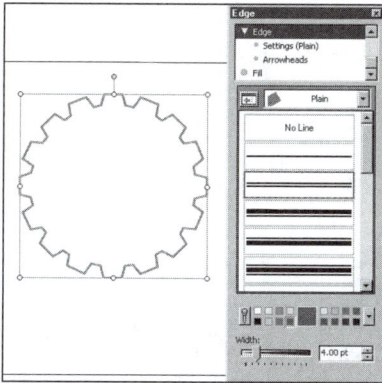

9.24

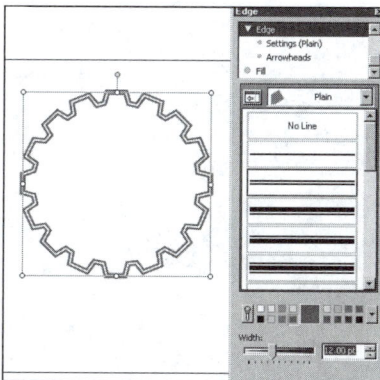

9.25

**Using a double
line instead of a
single one draws
more attention to
the fill inside the
lines.**

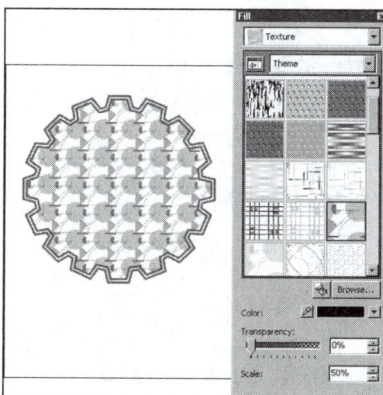

9.26

You can easily change the look of
objects, including many simple line-
art drawings, by changing the edges
and fills in an object. In this example, a simple geometric object is
changed dramatically in just a few
steps.

1. Select the object and open the
    Edge workpane
    (Format→Edge→Plain) **(9.24)**.

2. Select the Thin-Thin line and
    set the width to 12 points
    (9.25).

3. Select a fill from the
    Format→Fill→Theme Texture
    gallery **(9.26)**.

4. Change the scale of the fill by
    typing 25% in the Scale box on
    the Fill workpane.

(N)OTE

*This procedure might not yield the same
results with every kind of object. It works
best with simple line-art images.*

CHAPTER 10

You can apply a 3D special effect to any object in PhotoDraw, including text objects you've created and clip art you've enhanced. This special effect works particularly well on text objects but is not always as noticeable on other objects such as photographs. With a little experience, you'll develop your own guidelines about when to use this unique special effect to its best advantage.

APPLYING 3D EFFECTS TO IMAGES

After you've applied the special effect, you can alter the basic appearance of the object by changing certain settings, such as the edges and thickness of the object, to enhance the effect. A little experimentation will show you what effects work best on your images, but changing the edge of an image is a good way to make the image look more impressive. Another effect you'll want to try is changing the overall depth of the image by changing the bevel types. A deeper-looking image looks more 3D than one that is more shallow-looking.

Changing the fill of all, or a portion, of the object or even the shininess of the outer skin of the object can create an extra-special look for a 3D object. You can also make appearance changes by altering the rotation, tilt, and lighting of the object. This chapter takes you through all the procedures necessary to allow you to create your own unique 3D designs.

Converting a 2D Object to 3D

The first step in using the 3D effects is to take a 2D object such as a piece of clip art or a text object and add another dimension. You might like the change that the initial step makes to the object so much that you won't use some of the refinements of the effect. You can always go back and make other 3D changes later.

1. Select the image or object you want to apply the effect to.

2. Select Effects→3-D to open the 3-D workpane (10.1).

3. Scroll through the gallery of effects, and click on one to apply it to the object. PhotoDraw applies the effect (10.2).

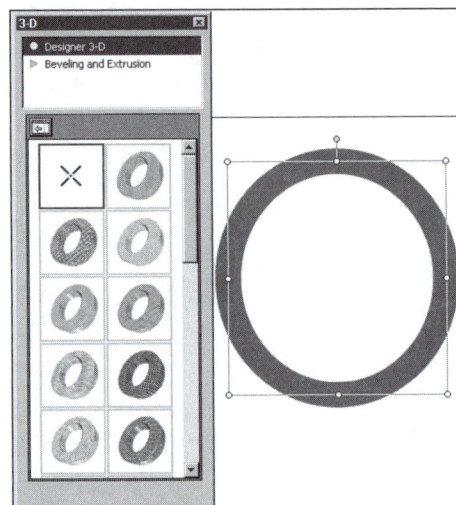

10.1

(N) O T E

If you don't like how the object looks after you've applied the 3D effect, click another effect to try it, or click the × in the upper-left corner of the workpane gallery to remove the 3D effect completely.

(T) I P

Depending on what piece of clip art you start out with, you might find the end result not as attractive as the original piece. If you start out with a simple shape without a lot of detail, you retain more of the original look of the image. In a more complex image, you get more radical changes.

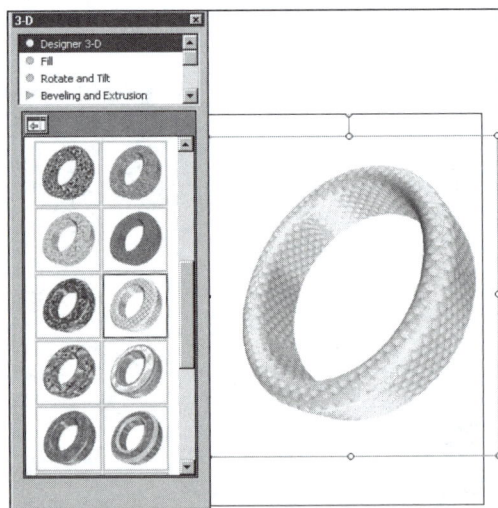

10.2

Applying a 3D Effect to a Text Object

10.3

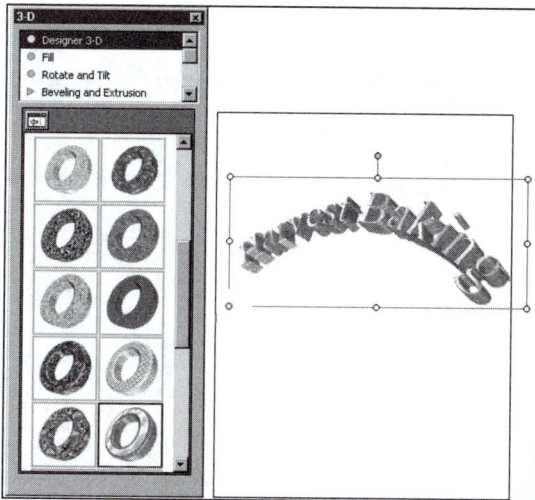

10.4 **After you have applied the 3D effect, you can alter the fill, rotation, tilt, and other aspects of the appearance.**

The 3D effect is particularly useful for adding interest to a plain text object or for making a piece of designer text look even more interesting. Because you often don't need to do anything more than apply the basic 3D effect, it's also a quick process to dress up some text by using 3D.

1. Create or select the text object you want to apply the effect to (10.3).

2. Select Effects→3D to open the 3-D workpane.

3. Scroll through the gallery of 3D effects. Click on the thumbnail to apply the effect (10.4).

(T) I P

If you want people to be able to read the text in the text object after you've applied the 3D effect, it's important to select only a subtle 3D effect. Too much rotation or distortion will make the text unreadable.

(N) O T E

It will be easier for people to see the details in the 3D effect if you select one that has more than one part, such as the Fluid Metal and Fig Ash one rather than the Canvas 3D effect.

Changing the Edges and Thickness of a 3D Object

After you've applied a 3D effect to a 2D object, you can change the look of the 3D effect by altering the thickness of the areas in the object, including the edges. Altering these settings is a good idea if you like the general look of a particular 3D effect but want to further enhance the look.

1. Apply the 3D effect to an object by choosing Effects→3D and then applying one of the effects in the 3D gallery. The 3-D workpane changes to show the list of editing options (10.5).

2. Click on Beveling and Extrusion from the list of options, and the workpane displays the gallery of available options (10.6).

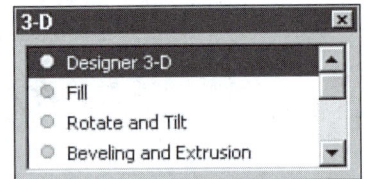

10.5

A bevel is the part of an object where two sides meet. You could also think of it as an edge.

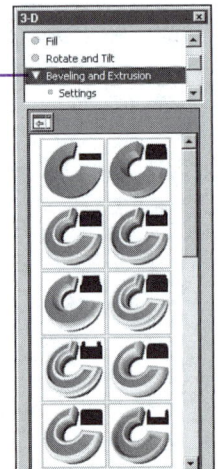

10.6

(T) I P

You can coordinate the look of a text object with a 3D object by using the fill in the 3D object to make a fill for the text object. [Click on the text object, select Format→Text, and select Designer Text from the Text workpane.] Click on the Eyedropper tool in the workpane and, using it, click somewhere on the nontext 3D object. PhotoDraw fills the text using color drawn from the 3D object.

10.7

10.8

3. To change the look of the bevel, scroll through the gallery of available bevel styles and select a bevel from the gallery by clicking on it (10.7).

4. To change the depth and width of the edges of the object, click on Settings under Bevel and Extrusion in the 3D workpane. Enter new numbers in the Bevel Depth and Width boxes.

5. To change the depth of the 3D effect on the entire object, enter a new number in the Depth box under Extrusion (10.8).

(N) O T E

PhotoDraw applies the 3D effect to the entire outer shape of an object—except for text objects. For these, it applies the 3D effect to each letter in the text object.

Using Special Effects on 3D Objects

Special effects available on the 3D workpane include changing the fill of an object, or part of an object, and changing the shininess of the object. Changing the fill allows you to use the general 3D effect but tailor the fill to make it more appropriate for your design or the nature of the object itself. Changing the shininess also can help change the appearance of depth of the object.

1. Apply the basic 3D effect to the object by choosing Effects→3D and selecting a 3D style for your object from the gallery in the 3D workpane.

2. Select Fill from the list of options in the 3D workpane to gain access to the Fill controls (10.9).

3. Click on one of the placement options to apply the fill to the face, edges, or sides of the object (10.10).

4. Select the type of fill you want to use by selecting from the drop-down list under the placement options. The work-pane changes to show the fill options available for that type of fill.

5. Make your fill selection from the gallery of options, and make any desired changes to the fill appearance by changing settings on the workpane (10.11).

You can fill a 3D object with a solid color, a texture, a designer gradient, a two-color gradient, or even a picture.

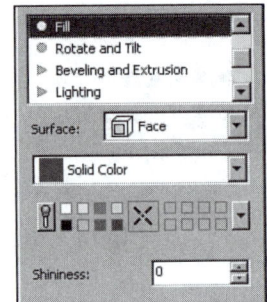

10.9

When changing all the fill areas on an object, work on a portion at a time. The fills used in the various placement positions do not have to be the same.

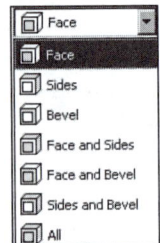

10.10

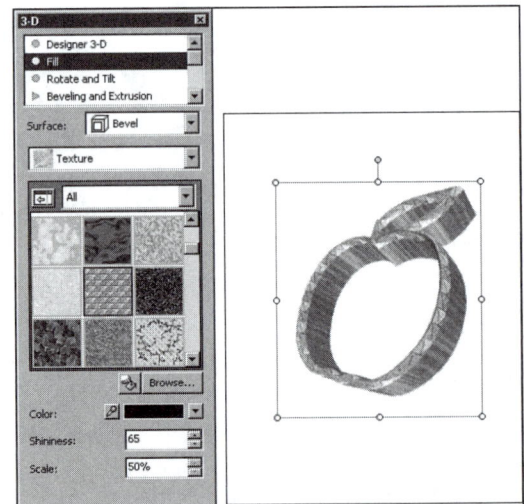

10.11

To make the 3D object look more metallic, increase the shininess setting by entering a higher number in the Shininess box on the 3D work-pane.

Changing the Rotation and Tilt of 3D Objects

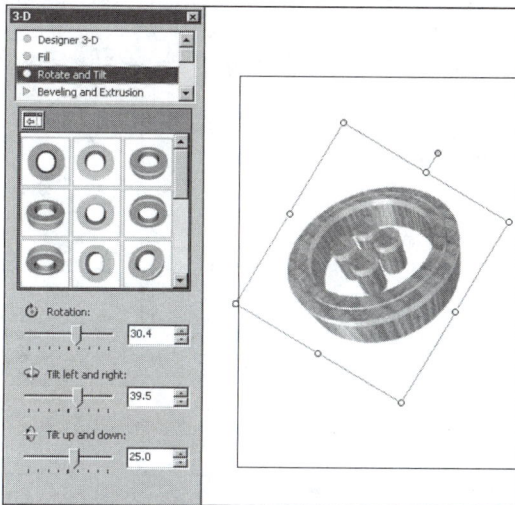

10.12   **Entering a negative number in the Tilt box causes the object to tilt downward. Entering a positive number tilts it upward. The degree of rotation (plus or minus) is limited to 180.**

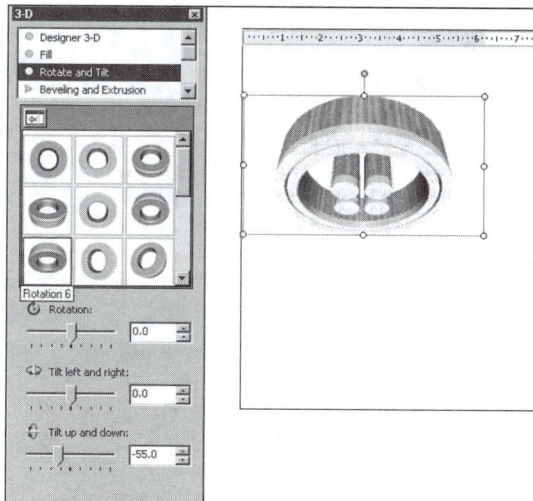

10.13

Changing the rotation and tilt of a 3D object is another way to customize a 3D effect. Implement these changes if you like the basic appearance of the effect but wish you could change the orientation of the 3D effect.

1. Select the 3D object you want to use by clicking on it.

2. Open the 3-D workpane by selecting Effects→3-D.

3. Select Rotate and Tilt from the list of 3D options. The rotate and tilt controls appear on the workpane (10.12).

4. Click on one of the examples in the gallery to apply that effect to the object (10.13). Click on the circle in the upper-left corner of the gallery to remove all rotation and tilt effects.

(N) O T E

You can also specify the rotation and tilt degrees by typing numbers in the boxes under the gallery.

(N) O T E

If you want to ensure that people can read your 3D text easily, go easy on the amount of tilt or rotation you use. Stay within a range of 15 to 25 degrees.

Using Lighting Effects on 3D Objects

Changing the lighting of an object can come in handy if you want to combine two or more objects and want to make one stand out more than the others. Simply change the lighting effect on one object to make it look much brighter than the others.

You can also apply a color wash to an object if you select a colored lighting effect. You can apply a rosy glow to almost anything this way.

1. Select the 3D object you want to use by clicking on it.

2. Open the 3D workpane by selecting Effects→3-D.

3. Select Lighting from the list of 3D options. The gallery of lighting effects opens (10.14).

4. Select an effect from the gallery to apply to your object, and PhotoDraw applies it automatically (10.15). To undo the effect, select Edit→Undo.

It's best to experiment with various examples in the lighting gallery because the result of a lighting effect on a 3D object can be slightly different from what's shown on the example in the gallery.

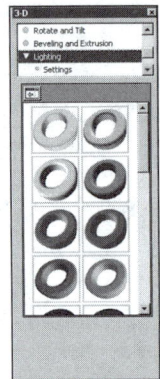

10.14

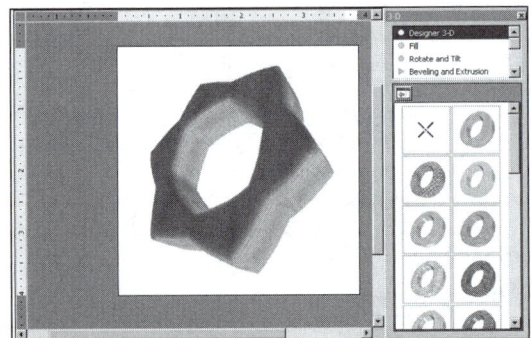

10.15 In this example of a 3D geometric shape, the lighting effects have been set so that one side of the shape is in deep shadow.

(N) O T E

As shown in this example, you can also change the look of the lighting on an object by changing the direction of the angle of the light and even the color of the light (10.16). To access these controls, select Settings under Lighting on the list in the 3D workpane.

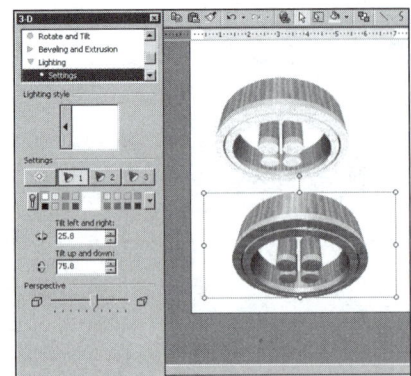

10.16

Combining 3D Effects with Other PhotoDraw Effects

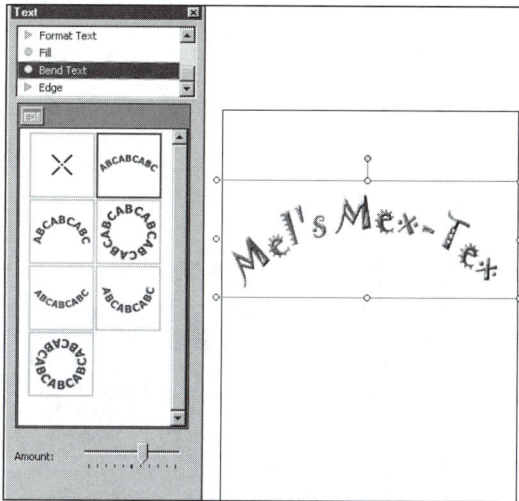

10.17   **This text was created using the Designer Text option called Designer Text 7.**

You can combine 3D effects with other PhotoDraw special effects to create unique objects and images. Here is one effective combination created using a Designer Text object coupled with another object using 3D special effects. Use your imagination to discover other combinations by following the same procedure with other objects.

1. Create a Designer Text object to incorporate into a design with your 3D object [see Chapter 2, "Creating and Editing Text Objects"].

2. Bend the text into a small arc **(10.17)**.

3. Apply a 3D effect to the text object by choosing Effects→3D and selecting a 3D style from the gallery **(10.18)**.

4. If desired, change the fill of the text object to add some additional style.

5. Change the tilt of the object to make it easier to read **(10.19)**.

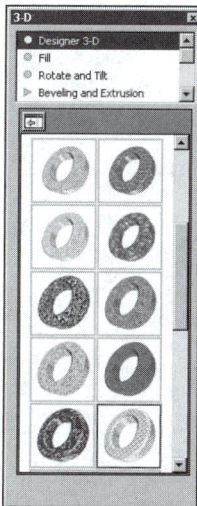

10.18

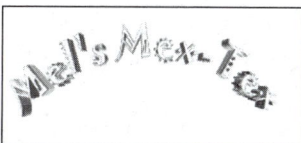

10.19

This example used a Designer Gradient multicolor fill to enhance the effect.

T I P

Don't bend text in a full circle if you intend to apply a 3D effect to the text object. If the 3D effect is too deep, the letters run into one another.

ⒸHAPTER 11

Shadows and transparency effects can add an air of mystery to images. Think of mists and shadows at sundown and you'll get the picture. They can also add an illusion of depth to a 2-D image, something that comes in handy when you want to add visual interest to an image.

CREATING SHADOW AND TRANSPARENCY SPECIAL EFFECTS

You can add shadows to almost any PhotoDraw object—you can add them to text objects, clip art, and cutouts of all kinds, including portions of photographs, and the actual photographs themselves.

The transparency and fade-out effects are useful for creating some interesting special effects. They are most useful if you want to blend two or more images to make them look as though they all belong together.

This chapter covers how to add shadows to an object and change the look and position of the shadow. You will find out how to change the look of an image by changing the amount of transparency it has; in addition, you'll learn how to add a fade-out effect to an object.

Adding a Shadow to an Object

1. Click on the object you want to add a shadow to in order to select the object.

2. Choose Effects→Shadow and the workpane of shadow effects appears (11.1).

3. Scroll through the gallery of available shadow effects until you find the one that suits your needs.

4. Click on the thumbnail example of the shadow you want to use, and PhotoDraw applies it to the selected object (11.2).

The × in the upper-left corner of the gallery of shadows enables you to remove a shadow effect you've added to an object.

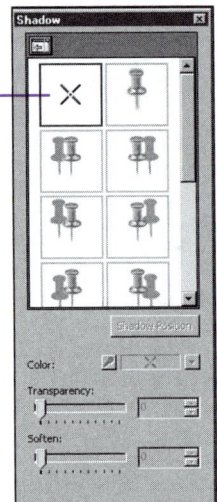

11.1

T I P

Be sure that the shadow you select does not extend beyond the edges of the page. If it does, resize the image or move the image with the shadow until all elements of the image are on the page.

N O T E

To make a shadow, PhotoDraw makes a copy of the outline of the selected object and fills the copy with light gray. If you want to make a shadow of a portion of an image, you must first cut out that part of the image or be sure that portion is a separate object.

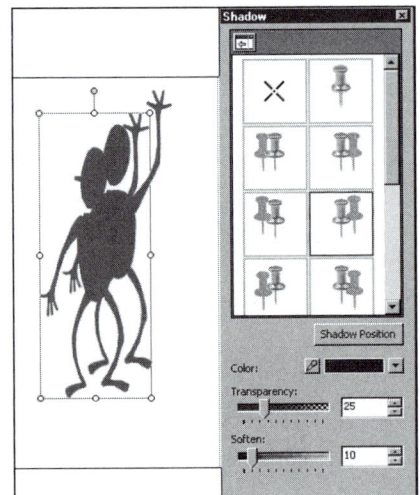

11.2

Changing the Position of a Shadow

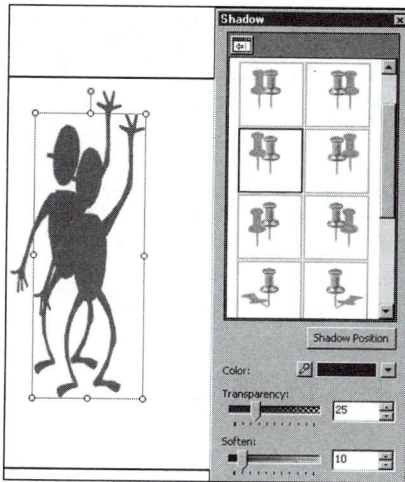

11.3

After you have applied a shadow to an object, you will find that it doesn't always present the depth or perspective on the object that you wanted. Changing the position and angle of the shadow is a good way to draw additional attention to the object and make good use of the shadowy effect. You can change the position of the shadow by using two different methods as described next.

1. Select the object with the shadow by clicking on it.

2. Select Effects→Shadow and the Shadow workpane appears.

3. Click on the thumbnail representation of the new shadow you want applied to the object. The shadow position changes to the new selection (11.3).

4. Another way to change the shadow position is to select the object and click on the Shadow Position button in the workpane.

continues

(N) O T E

Only one shadow effect can be applied to an object. PhotoDraw applies the effect as soon as you click on the thumbnail, enabling you to try the various options without committing to one immediately.

Changing the Position of a Shadow continued

5. The shadow is selected **(11.4)**, enabling you to move it to the desired position **(11.5)**.

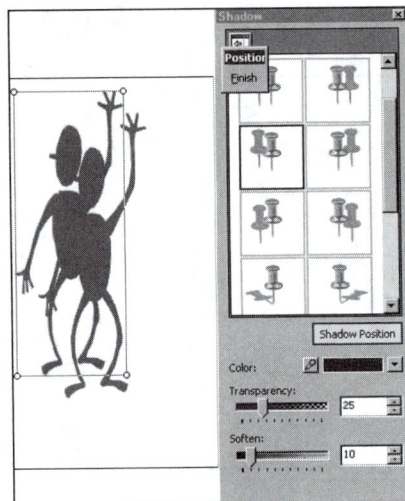

11.4

ⓉI P

To keep the shadow looking realistic, keep it near the object used to create the shadow. Move the shadow far away from the object if you are creating a special effect using the shadow.

Ⓝ O T E

If the end use of your image is a Web site, be careful with shadows. Although shadows will add dimension and enhance almost any Web site, you can run into trouble making your images float transparently on a background if they have shadows. If you're going to use shadows, your background should be a solid color, and you should incorporate that color into the background of your images before saving them in their final format. This will give you a cleaner-looking site.

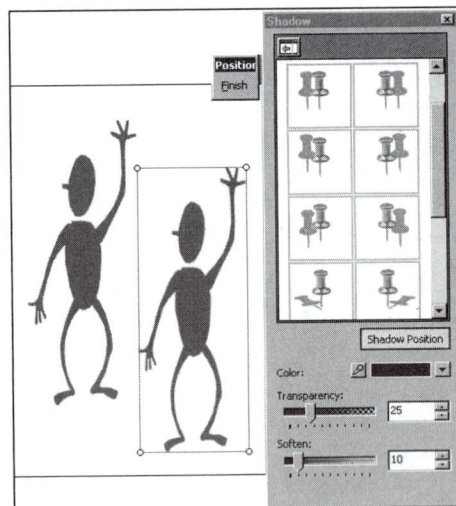

11.5

Using Color to Enhance the Shadow Effect

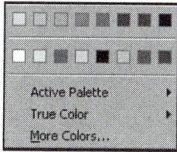

11.6

11.7   **By modifying the color, transparency, and soften variables on the shadow toolbar, you can create shadows that fit closely with the color scheme of your image, making it look authentic.**

After you've created a shadow, you can change the color of the fill of a shadow from light gray to another color. Shadows are normally shades of gray, but there's no reason you can't take liberties with the fill in shadows, unless you're trying to create a photo-realistic image. Try filling shadows with shades of blue or red or blends of colors—something more interesting than simple gray.

1. Click on the object with the shadow to select the shadowed object.

2. With the Shadow workpane open, click on the down arrow next to the Color list. A palette of available colors opens (11.6).

3. Click on the square for the color you want to use, and the shadow turns that color.

(T)I P

To further change the look of the shadow (11.7), you can use the Transparency and Soften controls (sliders and boxes) at the bottom of the workpane.

(N)O T E

You can select a color for the shadow from another object or part of the image by using the Eyedropper tool in the workpane to select the color.

Separating a Shadow from an Object

You can create a fun special effect by separating a shadow from an object and then placing objects between the shadow and the original object. In this example, the shadow has been separated from the main image, resulting in a "pretzel" box (11.8).

1. Click on the image with the shadow to select it.

2. Open the Shadow workpane (Effects→Shadow) and click the Shadow Position button.

3. Click on the shadow and drag it away from the object (11.9).

4. Make color or other appearance changes to the object as needed for your design.

5. Position another object between the original and its shadow to create a depth effect (11.10).

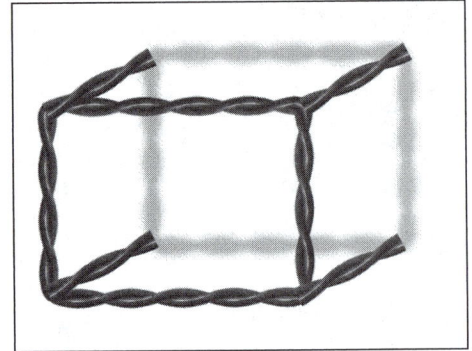

11.8

Click the Finish button on the floating toolbar when you have moved the shadow to its new location.

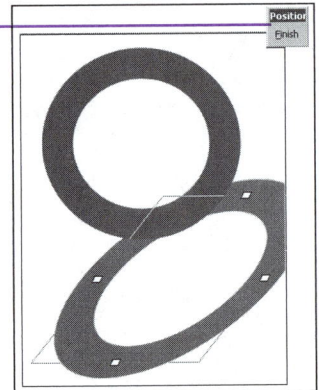

11.9

The primary limitation encountered as a result of style sheet positioning is the lack of browser support and backward compatibility.

You can't separate the object and its shadow to create two separate objects. If you want to make two versions of the same object, copy and paste the original and then change the appearance of the copy.

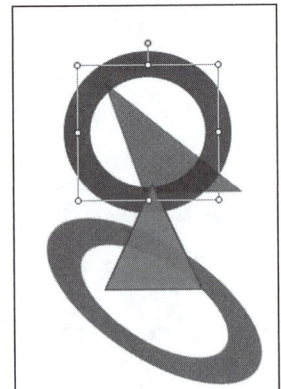

11.10

Changing an Object's Transparency

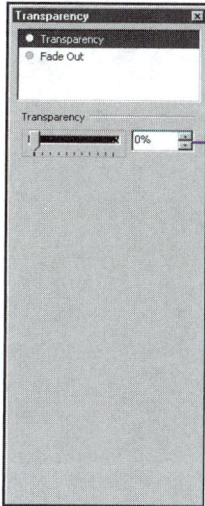

11.11

Don't set the Transparency level to 100% or the object will disappear.

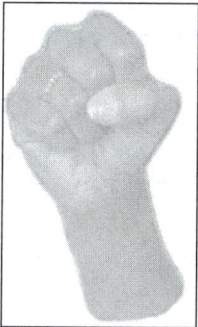

11.12

If you change the transparency of an object, you make it look translucent or even almost transparent. This is an artistic effect useful for layering objects or for combining several objects into one image. Objects placed under a transparent object can be seen through the transparent object.

1. Click on the object to select it.

2. Select Effects→Transparency and the Transparency work-pane appears (11.11).

3. To make the object more trans-parent, move the Transparency slider to the right or enter a higher value in the box.

4. To make the object less trans-parent, move the slider to the left or enter a lower value in the box.

(T) I P

For a ghostly look, make the object look almost transparent and then outline it with a solid color taken from the image or one that's two or three shades darker than the color in the image (11.12).

(N) O T E

If you want to change the transparency of part of an image, the part you want to change must be separated from the rest of the image. You can do this by creating it sepa-rately or by using the Cut Out function to select the area to change.

Changing the Fade-Out Characteristics of an Object

Fading out is a kind of transparency effect, but you use a different workpane to apply it. With a fade-out, you control how transparent the image is at the start and end of the effect. You can also control the direction of the fade-out.

If you set both sliders or numbers to 100%, the object will disappear.

1. Select the object you want to apply the effect to by clicking on the object.

2. Choose Effects→Transparency and the Transparency workpane appears.

3. Click on Fade Out and the workpane changes to show the Fade Out controls (11.13).

4. To make the start or end of the fade more transparent, move the appropriate slider to the right or enter a higher number in the box next to the slider (11.14).

5. To select a shape for the fade effect to move in, click on the left arrow next to the Shape box to open the Gallery of Shapes (11.15).

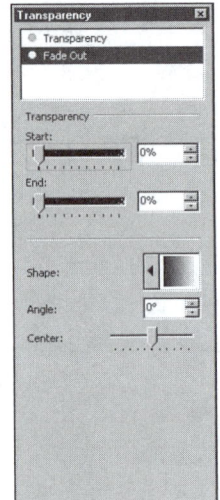

11.13

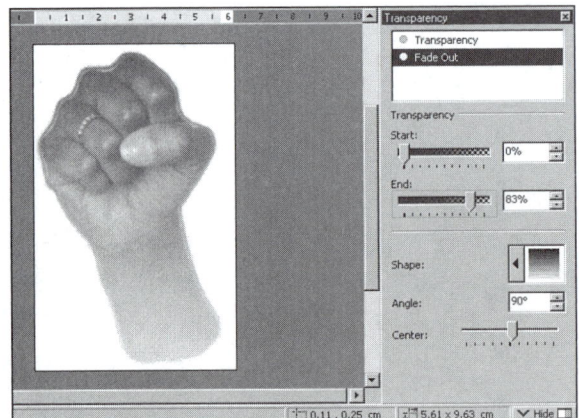

11.14

11.15 **If you consider all the possible combinations of Shape, Angle, and Center settings for the fade-out effect, you have thousands of options in this one special effect.**

(N) O T E

You can also open the Fade Out workpane by selecting Fade Out from the Effects menu (Effects→Fade Out).

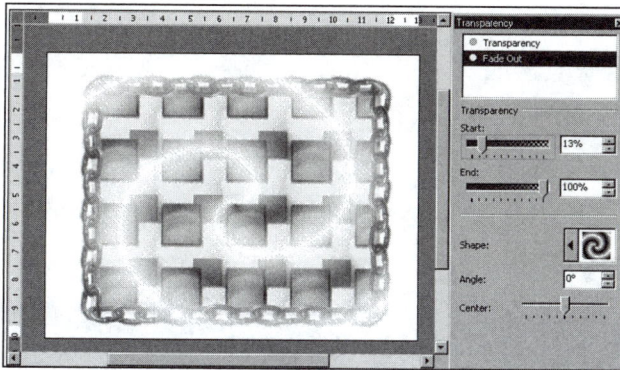

11.16

6. Click on a shape to select it. PhotoDraw applies the effect (11.16).

(N) O T E

To further alter the look of the effect, change the settings for Angle by entering another number in the degree box, or move the Center slider to the left or right—or make both changes.

(T) I P

To create a really unusual image, use the transparency effect on one object in a design and the fade-out effect on another.

©HAPTER 12

Because color is such an important tool for creating a great-looking image and PhotoDraw has so many ways to change colors in an image, it's worth the time to learn how to create and use custom color palettes and to make color selections and changes.

A color palette is a collection of colors. PhotoDraw comes with several ready-to-use color palettes, so you'll want to start a new design project by looking at these schemes first.

CUSTOMIZING COLORS FOR POWERFUL IMPACT

Later, you might want to create your own custom palette. After you have created a custom palette, you can save it with an image. That way, the palette goes along with the image and can be accessed by anyone else using PhotoDraw. Saving a custom color palette with an image is also a good way to change the colors in an image.

You can also export and import custom palettes—which makes it easy to share custom-created palettes with other people working on the same project. It also lets you select colors for use in a series of design projects.

After you've mastered the art of creating palettes, you'll want to use some of those palettes, and the standard color selections in PhotoDraw, to change colors in images, fills, outlines, and brushes. Those procedures, along with the methods of creating and working with custom color palettes, are covered in this chapter.

Using a Preset Color Scheme

If you need to select a set of colors to use for a project, your best bet is to start with one of the color schemes provided in PhotoDraw. Using these color-coordinated sets of colors can save you time, even if you use only a few colors from the set.

1. Click on any open image or object to start the process.

2. Select Format→Fill→Color Scheme to open the Fill workpane, and the More Colors window automatically opens to the Color Schemes tab (12.1).

3. Scroll through the list of available color palettes, and click on the name of the palette you want to use. The window changes to show the colors in the palette at the bottom of the window.

4. Click OK to close the More Colors window. The colors from the color scheme you selected appear in the small squares on the Fill workpane.

12.1

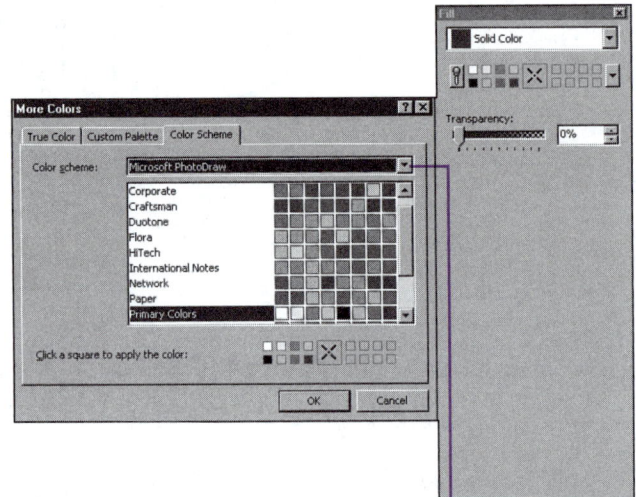

You can use color palettes from other Microsoft programs such as Microsoft Word and PowerPoint. Click on the down-arrow button in the top box in the More Colors window to change to these other palettes.

(T) I P

After you have selected a color scheme and the colors appear on the Fill workpane, you can use these colors as you would any solid fill. They will remain the default solid color fills until you select another color scheme.

Creating a Custom Color Palette

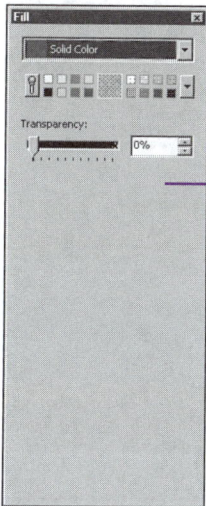

Any color workpane can be used to create an empty palette.

12.2

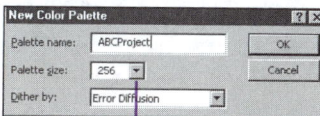

12.3 **After you set up a palette, you can't increase the number of colors in the palette. Select the largest palette size you'll need, or specify 256 colors if you're not sure how many you'll need.**

Custom color palettes are useful when you're working on a series of related images because they keep all the colors you've selected for an image in one palette. If you are working with other people on your project, a custom palette ensures that everyone is working with the same colors. To create a custom color palette, you must first create an empty palette and then fill the palette with your color choices.

1. Click on any open image or object to start the process.

2. Choose Format→Fill→Solid Color to open the Fill workpane (12.2).

3. Click the down arrow next to the color swatches and select More Colors from the drop-down list of colors and palettes.

4. Click the New button on the More Colors window. The New Color Palette window opens.

5. Type a name for the palette, and choose the number of colors you want in the palette and the type of dither pattern you want from the drop-down list of options (12.3). Click OK.

(N) O T E

continues

You can create an unlimited number of custom color palettes, but you cannot delete or change the palettes that come with PhotoDraw.

Creating a Custom Color Palette continued

6. The blank palette will now appear **(12.4)**. You can add colors to the new palette by clicking the Generate Colors button and choosing from the list of options in the Generate From drop-down list or by clicking the Import button and importing a color palette from another source **(12.5)**. See the next task on adding new colors to a palette for more details on generating colors from an existing image.

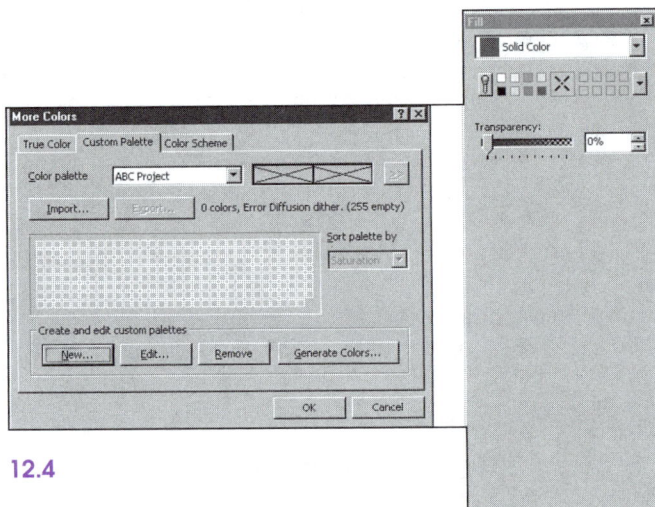

12.4

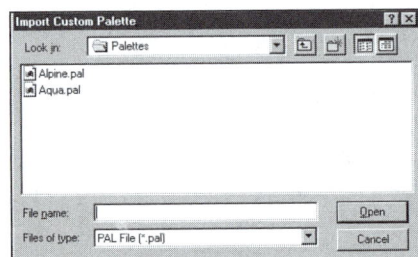

12.5

TIP

In the Dither By box, click the dithering option appropriate for your type of image. Error Diffusion works well with photographs if you can't display them in thousands of colors due to project limitations such as creating for the Web. Solids work better for clip art pictures with large areas of solid color.

TIP

When you need to match an exact color (when designing a brochure and you want it to match the company logo), try to find the exact RGB color value of the Pantone image from the original graphic designer or printer, and then enter the exact values into the RGB fields in the More Colors dialog box **(12.6)**.

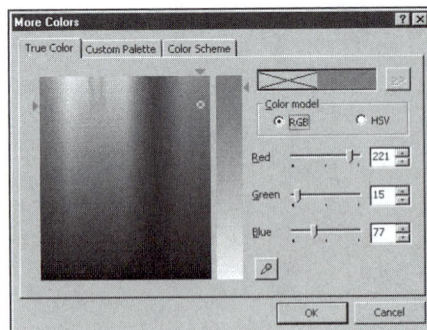

12.6

Adding New Colors to a Custom Palette

12.7

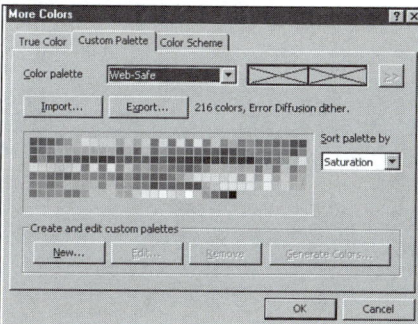

12.8

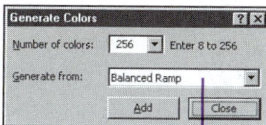

12.9 **You can generate colors automatically by selecting one of the color options listed in the Generate From drop-down list.**

After you've selected colors for a custom palette, it's possible that later you might find there are other colors you need to include in the palette. Instead of creating a new custom palette, you can just add them to the existing custom palette by using colors from an image.

1. Click on the image that contains the color or colors you want to add to the custom palette.

2. Open the Fill workpane **(12.7)** by selecting Format→Fill→ Solid Color.

3. Click the down arrow next to the color choices. The pop-up list of color choices and palettes opens.

4. Click on More colors and the More Colors window opens **(12.8)**.

5. Click on the Custom Palette tab, and select from the drop-down list of available palettes.

6. Click the Generate Colors button on the palette window. The Generate Colors window opens **(12.9)**.

continues

Adding New Colors to a Custom Palette continued

7. Enter the number of colors you want to add to the palette, then scroll to the bottom of the list of color sources to generate from, and select Picture (12.10). Click Add to start the process.

8. PhotoDraw adds the number of colors you specified from the existing picture.

9. To add more colors from other sources, repeat steps 6 through 8, choosing a different source from the list of colors (see step 7) until you have added all the colors you want. Click Close to end the process. You cannot have more than 256 colors in a palette.

You can also generate a palette by using colors in part of an image or object. Use the same procedure, but select only the desired portion of the image or object before starting the process, and choose Selection from the list of sources.

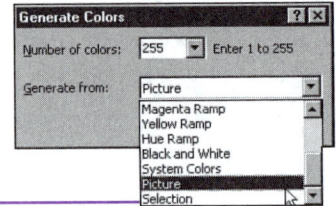

12.10

(N) O T E

Select System Colors to create a palette of the 20 basic colors in the Windows operating system. Select Balanced Ramp to create a palette with 216 entries of equal numbers of red, green, and blue entries.

(N) O T E

Be careful not to accidentally click the Remove button as it will completely remove your palette—not just one color—and you will have to re-create the entire palette.

Modifying a Custom Color Palette

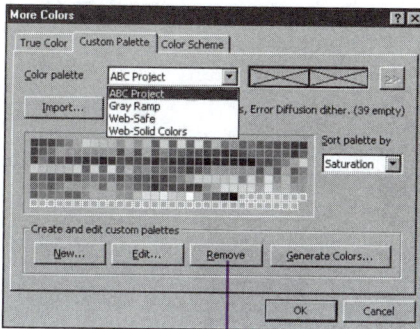

12.11 **While you are editing a custom color palette, do not click the Remove button unless you want PhotoDraw to discard the entire palette.**

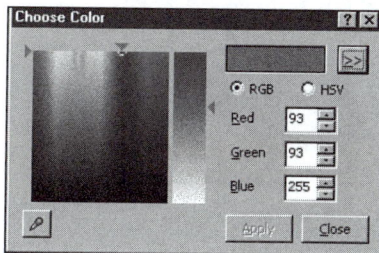

12.12

After you have created a custom color palette, you can change some (or all) of the colors in the palette. This feature comes in handy if color selections or specifications change and you want to update the palette.

1. Open the custom palette by selecting Format→Fill→Solid Color.

2. Click the down arrow next to the color swatches and choose More Colors. On the Custom Palette tab, select the custom palette from the drop-down list of available palettes (12.11).

3. Double-click on the color you want to change. The Choose Color window opens.

4. To select a color from the color matrix, click on the color (12.12).

5. To specify a color by using the RGB value, enter those values in the Red, Green, and Blue boxes.

continues

(N)OTE

If you want to arrange the colors in the palette from light to dark or some other order, click on the down-arrow button under the words Sort Palette By to bring up a list of sorting options.

Modifying a Custom Color Palette continued

6. To specify a color by using the HSV value, select HSV and enter the values in the Hue, Sat (Saturation), and Value boxes **(12.13)**.

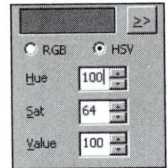

12.13

7. To specify a color by selecting one from an image, click on the Eyedropper tool on the Choose Color window and select the color **(12.14)**.

8. Click the Apply button to put the new color in the palette. Continue making color changes as needed and click the Close button to finish.

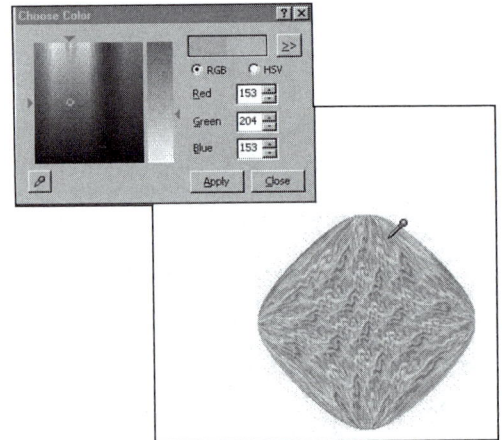

12.14

(T) I P

Using RGB and HSV values to create a color allows you to specify an exact color rather than guessing. Many color charts have RGB and HSV values you can use to select and create colors.

(N) O T E

To save time, you can create one master palette and then create secondary color palettes by importing the colors from the master palette.

Saving a Palette with an Image

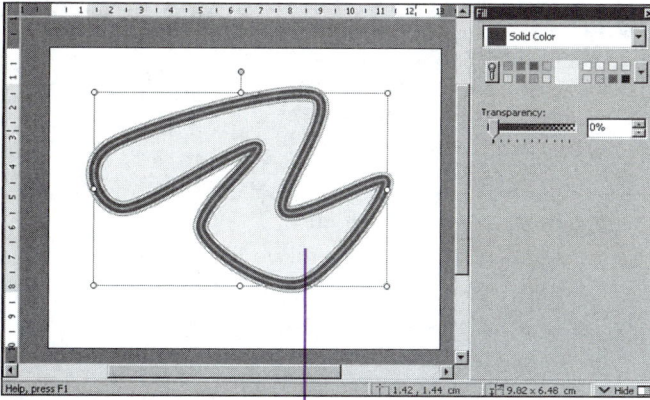

12.15 **This image has been filled with yellow from the custom Web-safe palette.**

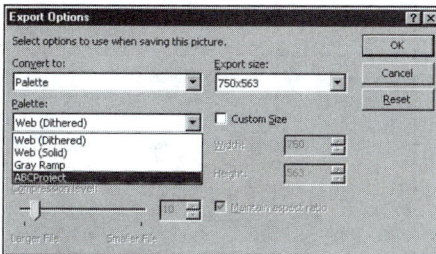

12.16

PhotoDraw enables you to apply custom palettes to an image by saving the file in a certain format and attaching the palette to that file. This is an easy way to apply the same palette to any number of images, such as ones you are going to use on the Web.

1. Click on the image to which you want to apply a custom palette (12.15).

2. Select File→Save As to open the Save As window.

3. Select one of the file formats GIF, PNG, PCX, TGA, BMP, or DIB from the drop-down list of Save As Type file formats.

4. Click the Options button and the Export Options window opens.

5. Select the new palette from the drop-down list of available palettes (12.16), and click the OK button to continue.

6. Click the Save button to save the file with its associated color palette. Enter a new name in the File Name box before clicking Save if you need to preserve the original file; otherwise, PhotoDraw simply overwrites the file with the new settings.

(N) O T E

If you are saving a file for use on the Web, be sure to save it as a GIF file.

Importing and Exporting Palettes

After you've created a custom palette, you might want to give it to someone else using PhotoDraw—or you might want to use a palette someone else has created. In order to share custom palettes, you'll need to know how to import and export PhotoDraw palette files (.pal).

1. Click on an image or object that uses the palette you want to export.

2. Choose Format→Fill→Solid Color to open a color work-pane.

3. Click the down arrow next to the color swatches and select More Colors from the drop-down list of color choices (12.17) to open the More Colors window.

4. To import a palette, click the Import button and locate the palette file you want to import (12.18). Click Open to finish the import process.

5. To export a palette, click the Export button and the Export Custom Palette window opens (12.19).

6. Select your file destination and rename the file, if desired. Click the Save button to export the palette.

Palettes are also useful for print publications—if you define a series of set colors that work well with your corporate image, you can email others the custom palette and instruct them to use only document colors that are from your custom palette. This will ensure visual integrity across all documents.

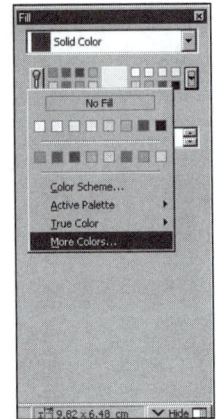

12.17

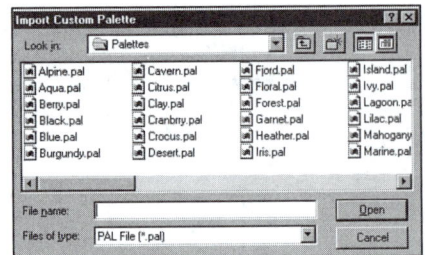

12.18

To save time during this process, before you start, find out the name of the custom palette you want to import and where it is located on your hard disk or server.

If you're working on a project with other contributors, it is wise to save custom palettes in a central location such as a network server.

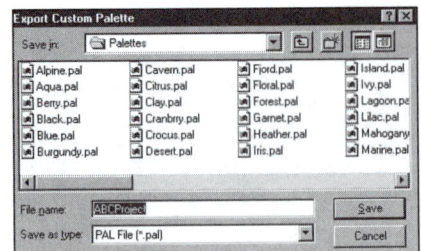

12.19

Changing Solid Fill Colors

12.20

12.21

Unless you've already chosen a color scheme, PhotoDraw doesn't remember the fill color you used the last time you filled an object, although it does remember the color used for the last outline. You have to specify a fill color or type each time you use any kind of fill. If you choose the wrong color and need to change it, or want to change the color later, it's an easy process.

1. Select an object to change by clicking on it (12.20).

2. Select Format→Fill→Solid Color, and the Fill workpane opens (12.21).

continues

(T) I P

The steps here are for changing solid fill colors. You can apply the same steps to other fill types by selecting the appropriate fill from the Fill pop-up menu and following the procedure outlined here.

Changing Solid Fill Colors continued

3. If the color you want to use is shown in the small squares below the list of fill types, click on the square **(12.22)**.

4. To see your other color choices by looking at the active color palettes, click the down-arrow button at the far right of the color selection area. A window with more color choices and a list of palettes opens.

5. Click on the More Colors button to get to the custom palettes and TrueColor control palettes **(12.23)**.

6. Click on the color you want to use, or create it by using the color controls; PhotoDraw applies the color choice.

The small squares at the left of the large square that displays the selected color are available colors. The squares to the right of the selected color box are empty until you select a fill color. Then, PhotoDraw fills them with shades of the color you've selected.

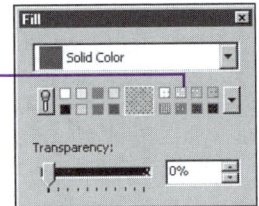

12.22

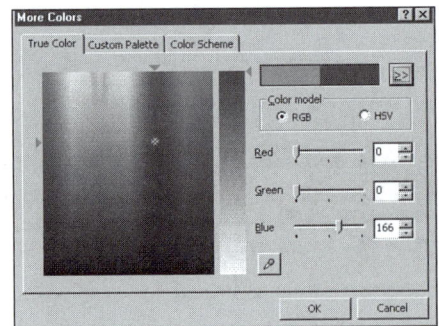

12.23

NOTE

The colors in the left squares are the colors you have used most recently or are colors in the color scheme you used last. PhotoDraw keeps them handy for you to use if you want to keep using the same colors.

Changing a Single Color in an Image

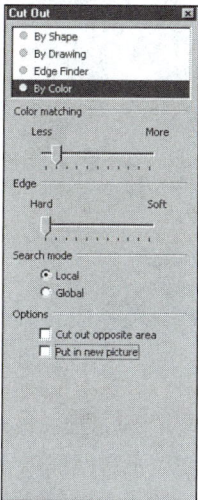

12.24

You can change the colors in an image by saving it with a custom color palette, but sometimes you might want to change the color of a fill in only one or two areas of an object. There are several ways to change one color at time in an object; this task covers one of the more common methods.

1. Select the object you want to change by clicking on it.

2. Select Tools→Cut Out and the Cut Out workpane appears **(12.24)**. (See Chapter 1 for other uses of cutouts in PhotoDraw.)

3. Choose By Color and be sure that the option Put in New Picture is not selected.

continues

(N) O T E

Unless you click on the object before accessing the Tools menu, the Cut Out option will not appear on the menu.

(T) I P

If the area where the color appears is small, zoom in on the area until you can see more of the color. That way, you'll get the color you want the first time, every time.

Changing a Single Color in an Image continued

4. Click on the areas where you want a new color to be inserted **(12.25)**.

5. With the Cut Out workpane still open, open the Fill workpane by selecting Format→Fill and then selecting the type of fill you want to use. The Cut Out workpane is replaced by the Fill workpane **(12.26)**.

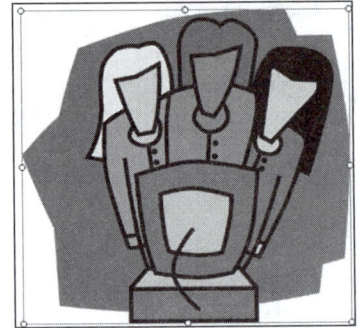

12.25

6. Select the fill you want to use by clicking on it, and PhotoDraw replaces the area with the fill or color you've selected **(12.27)**.

7. Hold down the Shift key, and click on the area you've changed and the object itself to select both.

8. Group the two by choosing Arrange→Group. The color changes are now part of the original image.

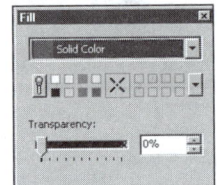

12.26

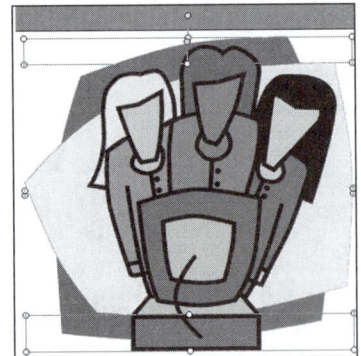

12.27

(N) O T E

PhotoDraw temporarily highlights the area you've selected in another color to show you which areas have been selected. This is not the final fill color, so don't worry about it.

(N) O T E

The grouping action at the end is necessary to combine the new color layer and the original image into one new image.

Copying Colors from Other Images

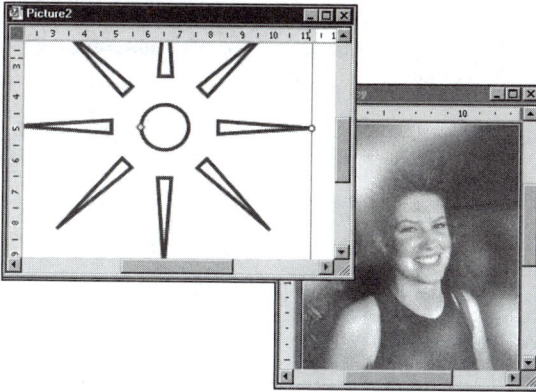

12.28

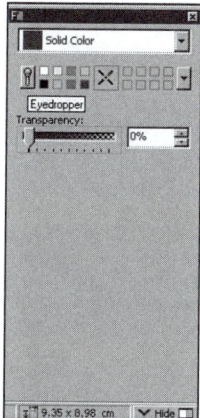

12.29

You might see a color in a photograph or piece of clip art that you would like to use in another image or put in a custom color palette. PhotoDraw lets you do that easily through the use of a nifty tool called the Eyedropper. You will see the Eyedropper on many PhotoDraw workpanes, and it always works the same way—it enables you to sample a piece of an image and use that sample to fill other areas or objects.

1. Open the image you want to use a color from and the image you want to use the color in **(12.28)**.

2. Click on the object you are going to use the color in to select the object.

3. To open a color workpane, select Format→Fill→Solid Color, and the Fill workpane opens **(12.29)**.

continues

(T) I P

You can open two windows or place the two objects temporarily in the same design. Placing two objects in the same design and deleting one later is easier if the objects are small enough to fit together on one design sheet, but because this is often not the case, you should align two windows as in Figure 12.28.

Copying Colors from Other Images continued

4. Click on the Eyedropper tool located to the left of the color swatches.

5. Click on the color in the other image that you want to use in the current image.

6. PhotoDraw applies the color to the selected image **(12.30)**.

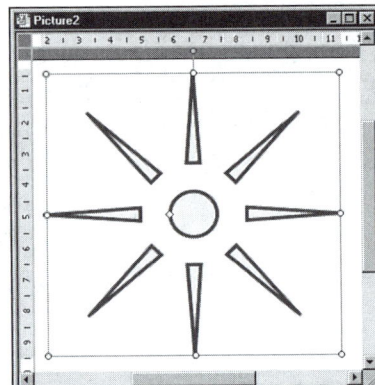

12.30

Ⓝ **O T E**

The cursor changes into an eyedropper after you have clicked on the Eyedropper icon.

Ⓝ **O T E**

This procedure applies color to an entire object, so it's best used for applying color to black-and-white line art or drawing objects.

Setting Brush Colors

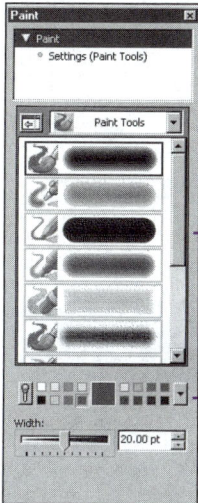

You can change the colors of the paint tools, as well as the shapes of the paintbrushes, on the workpane.

12.31

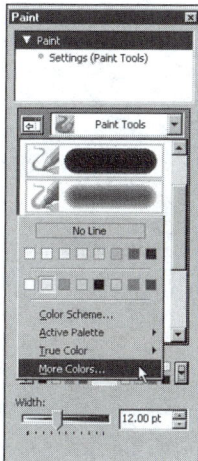

12.32

Artists sometimes use a whole range of brushes—some big, some little—each providing the artist with a different brush effect. PhotoDraw lets you mimic those effects by providing dozens of brush types, shapes, and sizes.

1. Choose Tools→Paint Tools to open the Paint workpane with the gallery of paint tools displayed (12.31).

2. Select a color for the brush by clicking on one of the small color swatches to the left or right of the large color square.

3. If the color you want to use is not visible, check the other palettes by clicking on the down-arrow button to the far right of the swatches and selecting a new palette to choose from (12.32).

(T) I P

You can also use the Eyedropper tool to select a color from another source, such as another image or your desktop, to use for the brush.

(N) O T E

You can change the width of the brush stroke by adjusting the Width slider at the bottom of the workpane. By changing the width, you can create a "layered" or depth effect: Use a narrower width first and then add more strokes using a wider width over the top of the original "layer."

ⓒHAPTER 13

These days, everyone (it seems) has a Web page or needs to put one together in a hurry. Fortunately, PhotoDraw lets you create many of the graphical elements you'll need for a Web page. These elements include sidebars, thumbnails, buttons, banners, and even background tiles. You won't need anything but PhotoDraw to create a whole set of graphic elements for your Web site.

CREATING WEB GRAPHICS

Because PhotoDraw uses templates, you can have a consistent look and feel for your graphics—your banners, buttons, and sidebars will work together in harmony. A common mistake for beginning Web designers is to incorporate all the "neat" things they find on the Web—which results in wildly inconsistent visuals on their Web site. Better yet, with PhotoDraw you can use a Theme style, which ties directly into the Themes of Microsoft FrontPage 2000. For example, if you've built your Web site using the Sumi theme in FrontPage 2000, you can add new banners, navigation, and backgrounds all using the Sumi style.

PhotoDraw's strength at Web graphics comes from its streamlined approach—the templates are all professional-looking, and require only your text input before they can be used. However, because the graphics are modular, you can replace key elements such as backgrounds to alter the entire look of the graphic.

Creating a Thumbnail

Thumbnails are smaller versions of larger, more detailed images that you might want to present on your site. You'll often find these on artists' or photographers' Web sites, or on a retail site where thumbnails of products in a catalog can be clicked on to bring up the corresponding full-size image. The reason for providing thumbnails linked to the larger images is that you can show many images at once without making the Web site visitor sit for what seems like forever waiting for large image files to download. To create a thumbnail—a miniature version of a PhotoDraw image to use on a Web page—you can use the Save for Use In Wizard.

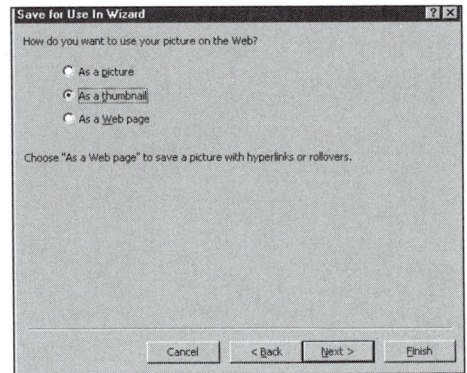

13.1

1. Open the file you want to save as a thumbnail, and select File→Save for Use In to activate the Save for Use In Wizard (13.1).

2. Select On the Web and click the Next button.

3. Select As a Thumbnail and click the Next button to continue.

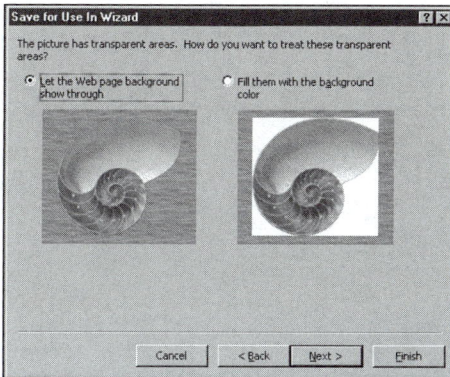

13.2

13.3

4. Click the Let the Web page Background Show Through check box to make the background of the graphic transparent **(13.2)**. Depending on the type of graphic you are using, you might choose the Fill Them with the Background Color check box to have the background of the image filled with the color that was in the image file. Click the Next button.

5. Review your file information and then click the Save button to finish using the wizard **(13.3)**. Enter a filename in the Save As window to save the file. PhotoDraw automatically saves the file in the GIF format.

(N) O T E

If you are not already in a wizard, you can also use File→Save As to save a file as nearly any type. For Web use, select GIF or JPEG. Click the Options button to see options for each image type. In the case of JPEG images, this includes resizing and compression level. For Web images, don't go over a JPEG compression level of 15—if you do, the quality of the image will degrade rapidly.

Creating a Button

Even if you don't like the appearance of the Web graphics created with the templates, using a template is still the fastest way to create a graphic. After you've created one, it's fairly easy to change the appearance to fit your needs. In this example, you will learn how to use a template to create a button for a Web page and then change the look of the button.

1. Activate the templates by selecting File→New from Template. The Templates workpane appears. Choose Web graphics from the drop-down list of template types (13.4).

2. Double-click on a button icon to bring up the gallery of choices (13.5).

3. Double-click on one of the buttons in the gallery to move to the next step in the wizard.

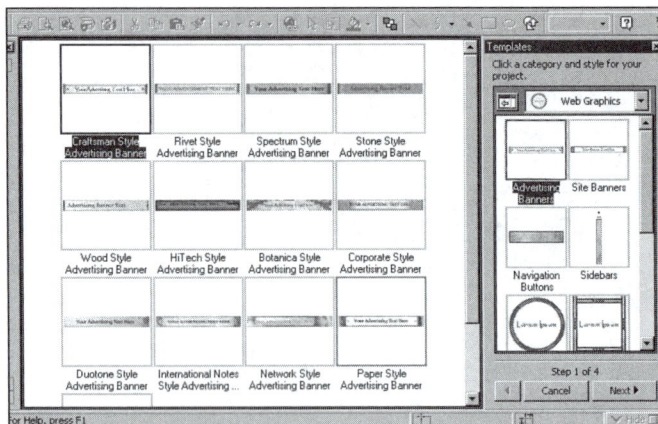

13.4

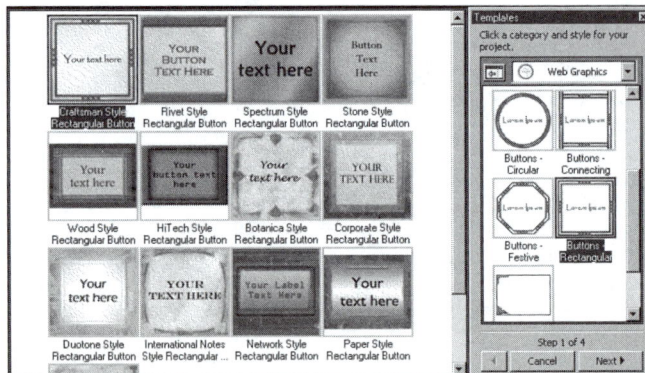

13.5

Ⓝ O T E

If you are going to replace the fill inside the button with something other than a standard PhotoDraw fill, save time by knowing where that replacement image file is before you start using the wizard.

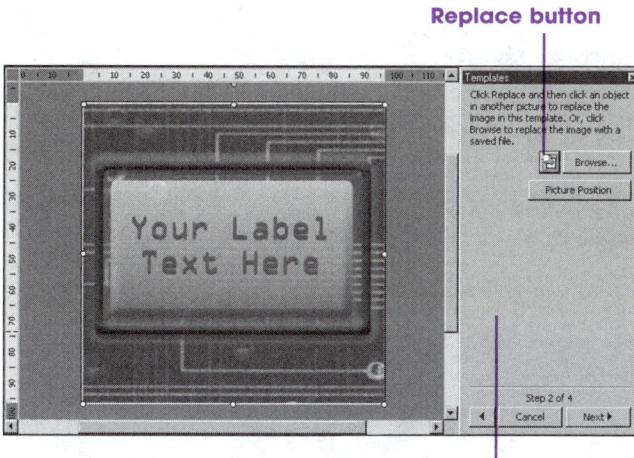

Replace button

13.6

You can also change the fill of the
button after you've created it by
using one of the preset fill options.

13.7

After you've entered your text, you can also change the
font, font style, and size. If you've created buttons previously for a Web site using PhotoDraw 2000, you'll want to
match the original style as closely as possible.

4. If desired, replace the fill on
   the button by clicking the
   Replace button or by using the
   Browse button to locate an
   image saved to disk **(13.6)**.

5. Click Next, and then replace
   the placeholder text on the button with new text **(13.7)**. Finish
   the wizard by clicking the Next
   button twice.

(N)OTE

*You can create other buttons and banners for
use on Web pages by following the procedure
outlined previously. Just choose the appropriate image type in the wizard.*

(T)IP

*If you find that the text on the buttons
(or other Web graphics) is hard to read when
the text or the object is reduced, select the
text portion of the image and clear the
Smoothing setting (under Text Flow on
the Text workpane).*

Creating Other Web Graphics by Using the Web Wizard

If you like the Web objects you can create by using the wizard but you need more objects than buttons or banners, you can create your own objects and coordinate them with others you made with templates by using the same fills. Here's how to create a divider by using one of the Web wizard fills.

1. Select File→New from Template and choose Web graphics from the drop-down list of categories. Choose rectangular buttons for the type of graphic you want to create.

2. Choose your button by double-clicking on the sample image, and click Next to move to step 3 of the wizard without changing the fill.

3. Delete the placeholder text from the button, and click Next two times to complete the wizard (13.8).

4. Select File→Picture Setup to open the Picture Setup window (13.9). Enter the new value of the divider you want.

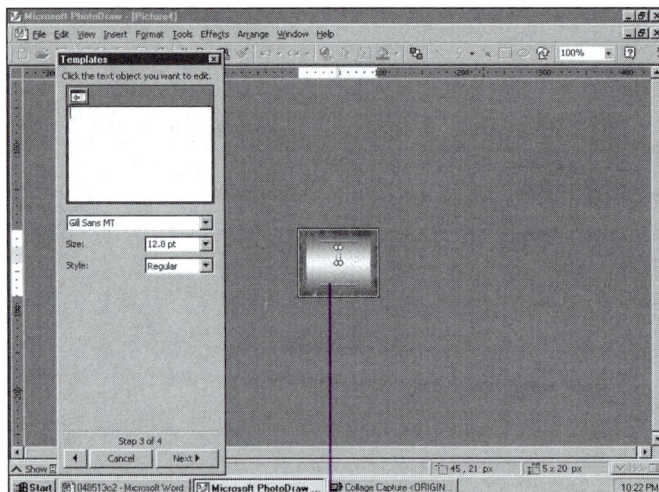

13.8   **A rectangular button without text can also be used to create backgrounds for button bars.**

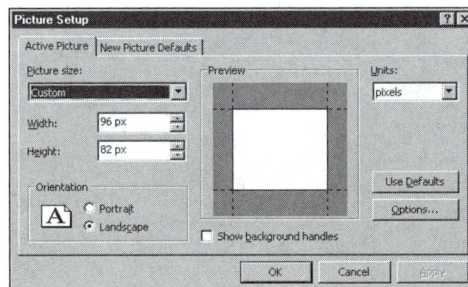

13.9

(N) O T E

If you do not change the picture setup to match the dimensions of the divider, PhotoDraw saves the area around the divider as part of the image, and that area will appear on the Web page, too.

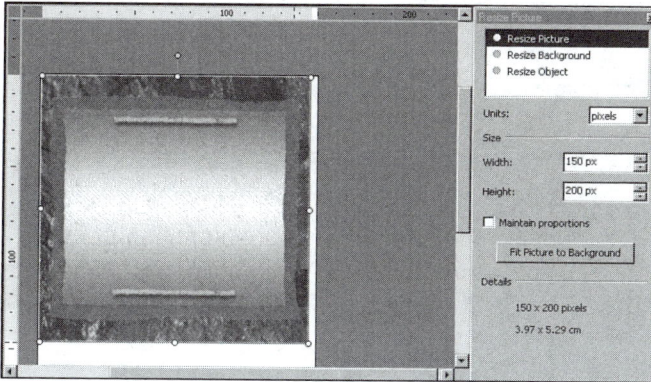

13.10

5. To tweak the image so that it's exactly the size you need, enter the pixel dimensions of the divider in the Width and Height boxes or click the Fit Picture to Background button. This will force the image to be resized to the background size. Be sure to save the image you've created before moving on to other work.

(T) I P

You can also resize the button manually. To do so, click on one of the small side or corner circles and drag the side or corner until the image is the length and width of the divider you need **(13.10)**. *Use the rulers and guides on the screen to help you size the graphic.*

Creating a Background Tile

To fill in the backgrounds of Web pages, designers sometimes use a background tile—a small graphic that Web-browser software displays repeatedly to fill the screen area— rather than using just a color in the background. This approach can provide you with more designing power when you're creating your Web site and give you a distinct look that will set your site apart from many others.

1. Click the New button in your toolbar to open a blank workspace. Draw a 2×2-inch square (Tools→Draw Tools). Use the Rectangle tool and hold down the shift key to get a constrained square. Select a thin line from the Edge workpane to draw the shape with. After the line is drawn, select No Line as the edge type.

2. Choose Format→Fill→Texture to fill the square with a textured fill (13.11).

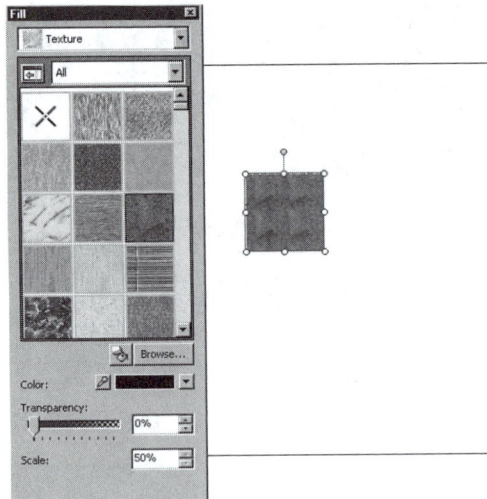

13.11

Because backgrounds on Web pages shouldn't dominate the design of the page, make the background tile lighter by setting the transparency level between 50% and 90%.

(T) I P

If you have created buttons or banners by using the Web graphics Wizard, you can use the Eyedropper tool on the Fill workpane to fill the background tile with a color sampled from one of these images.

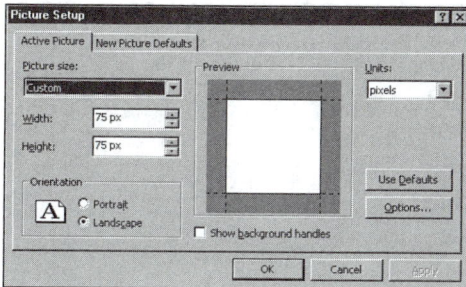

13.12

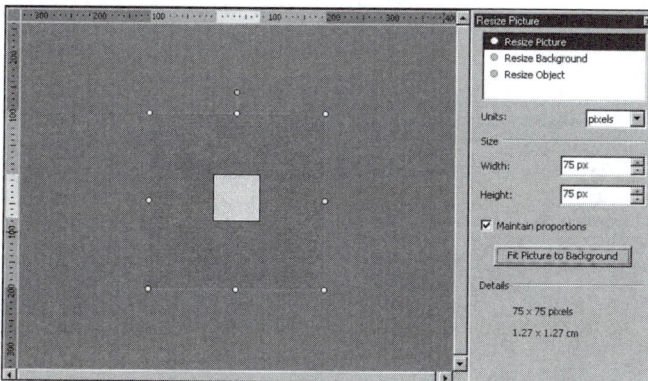

13.13

3. Select File→Picture Setup to open the Picture Setup window. Change the units to pixels and enter 75 for the width and height (13.12). Click OK and Apply to change the page size.

4. Resize the square by right-clicking on it, and choosing Resize. On the right toolbar, click Fit Picture to Background. This will shrink the image to fit the new background size (13.13).

5. Save the image as a JPEG file.

Ⓝ O T E

If you want to use the tile as the background for your Windows computer, save the file as a BMP (bitmap) file.

Ⓝ O T E

You can create various background tiles in PhotoDraw by using this procedure. Simply use the image or fill of your choice instead of a textured fill, as used here.

Creating a Banner Without Using a Wizard

You can create a Web-page banner without using a wizard. Use the wizard when the sample button is exactly (or almost exactly) what you are looking for. However, if you want to create something entirely original, use the banner template instead of the Web Graphics Wizard.

1. Select File→New to open the New window. Click on the Pictures tab and double-click on the Banner icon (13.14).

2. Open the image file you want to use to fill the background of the banner.

3. Select Tools→Cutout to cut out a strip from the image that has the same dimensions as the banner (13.15).

The default banner size is 4 inches long by 0.43 inch tall. Change the dimensions by using File→Page Setup if you want a different size.

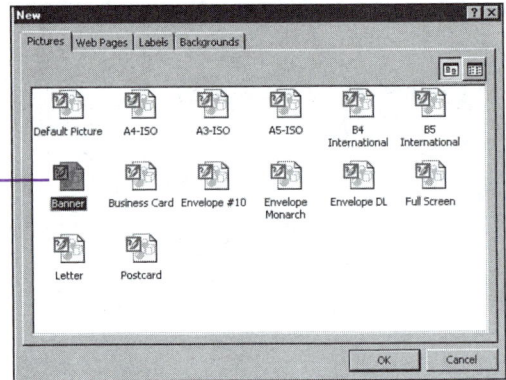

13.14

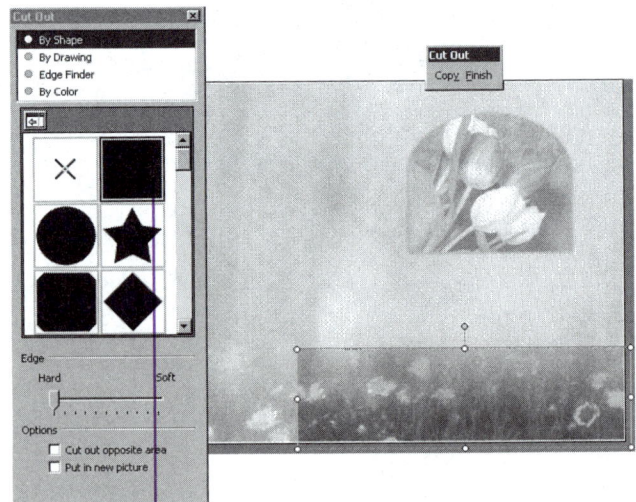

13.15

To create a rectangle cutout, use the square cutout shape and resize it into the rectangle size you need.

(T) I P

Use the cutout method if you want to keep the dimensions present in the portion of the image you are using in the banner. (See Chapter 1 for information on creating cutouts.) Resize an image to fit the banner size if you don't care about the dimensions or proportions.

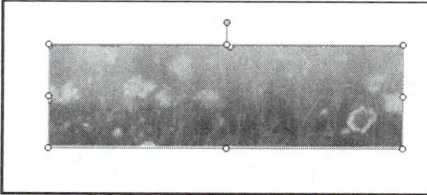

13.16

4. Copy and paste the strip onto the banner shape (13.16).

5. Add text or other images to the banner as desired (13.17).

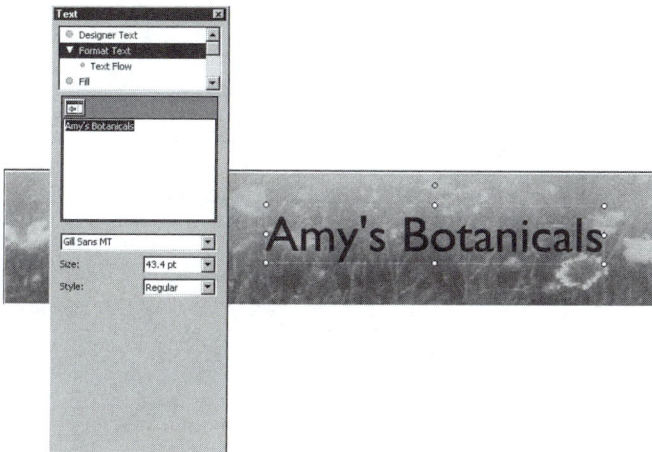

13.17

(N)OTE

PhotoDraw comes with a collection of images called Web Art that you can use to create background tiles and banners as outlined in this chapter.

Saving a Web Graphic with Transparent Areas

Web graphics placed on top of back-grounds or other page elements must have transparent areas if you want the material underneath to show through; otherwise, you will have a white area surrounding your image. PhotoDraw lets you create transparent areas in graphics when you save the image as a GIF file.

1. Open the image that you want to have a transparent back-ground, and select File→Save for Use In to activate the Save for Use In Wizard (13.18).

2. Select On the Web and click the Next button.

3. If your image has areas which can be made transparent, the wizard asks whether you want to have the background show through. Select the Let the Web page Background Show Through option (13.19), and click the Next button.

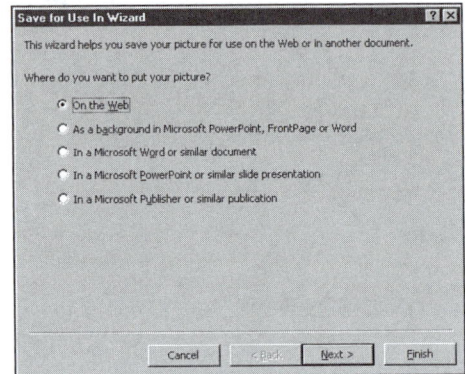

13.18

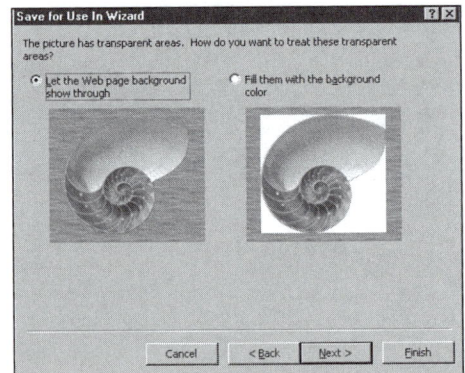

13.19

(N) O T E

If your graphic doesn't have large areas of whitespace (or another solid color), you won't see this step in the wizard. PhotoDraw looks at your image and makes an educated guess about whether or not it can be made transparent. There is no way to force it to accept transparency.

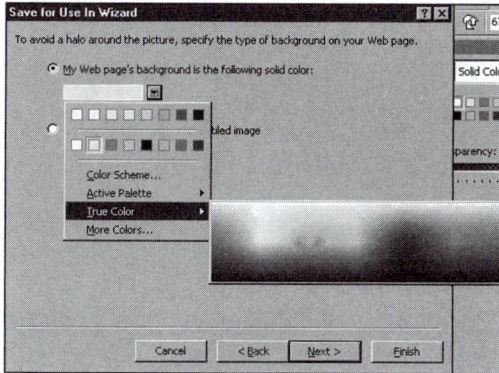

13.20

4. Select the color or type of back-
   ground you are using for the
   Web page (13.20). Click the
   Next button.

5. Click the Save button to save
   the file.

NOTE

*If you know you don't have transparent
areas in your GIF image, you can save a little time by not using the wizard. Use
File→Save As to save the image as a GIF
file. If you use these options, you can't save
the file with transparent areas.*

©HAPTER 14

In this chapter you will learn how to...

Create a New Category

Add Images to the Clip Gallery

Change or Delete a Category

Restore Deleted Categories or Image Clips

Open Multiple Categories

Use Keywords to Search for Images

Add Keywords for Searching

The Clip Gallery that comes with PhotoDraw is a good way to keep at your fingertips all the images you create or use in your projects. You can also find images in the Clip Gallery by using keyword and visual searching methods.

Because you can import files saved in any file format PhotoDraw supports, you can use the Clip Gallery as a digital media resource bank for all the still images you use on a regular basis, as well as for digital sound and video clips.

WORKING WITH THE CLIP GALLERY

You can add previews for images you have created or add previews for ready-to-use images such as other clip art collections. You can organize the previews into categories and assign properties to allow you to quickly find the images you want. You can even open the Clip Gallery without launching PhotoDraw so that you can import images you've created or edited with PhotoDraw into other Microsoft applications.

Creating a New Category

Create a new category for each project and add your images to this category as you create them. This way, you'll always be current with your image inventory, and it will be easier to share images with others.

1. With a document started, Open the Clip Gallery (Insert→Clip Art) and click on the New Category icon. Enter the name of the new category in the New Category window that appears (14.1), and click OK.

2. PhotoDraw places the new category in the collection of categories in the correct alphabetical location and moves the screen to the location of the new category (14.2).

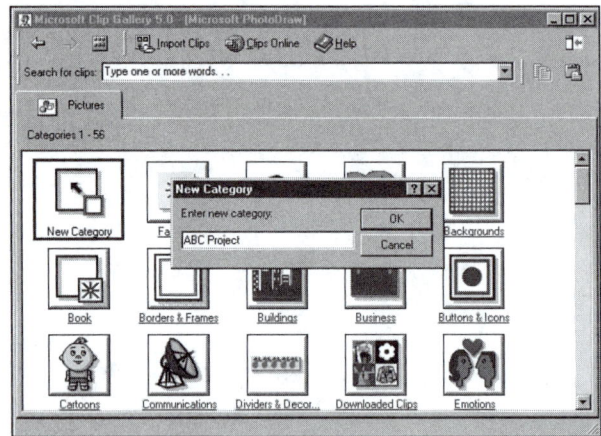

14.1

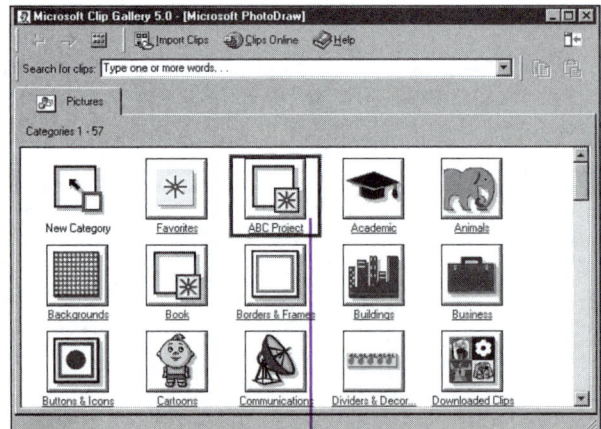

14.2   **The new category's icon appears with the name of the category under it.**

T I P

Choose a category name that is both descriptive of the images in the category and easy for you and others to remember.

T I P

If you pick a category name that's already taken, you'll receive an error message. Try using an alternative form—if it's a business category, try using "Business–Company Art" or something similar.

Adding Images to the Clip Gallery

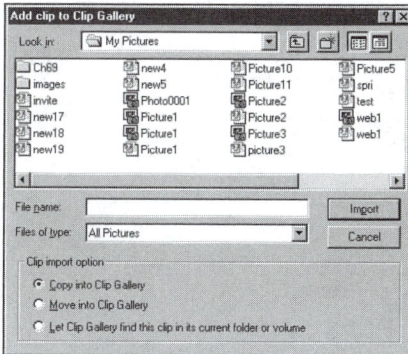

14.3

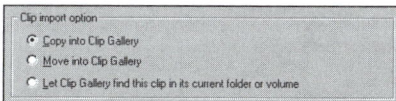

14.4

PhotoDraw displays all supported image types.

PhotoDraw lets you add images you create or images from other sources to the Clip Gallery. You can create new categories in the Clip Gallery to add your images into, or you can add them to the preexisting categories that come with Clip Gallery. You can even access the same image file in different categories by adding the file to more than one category.

1. With an image file or blank page open, choose Insert→Clip Art to gain access to the Clip Gallery.

2. Click Import Clips at the top of the window, and the Add Clip to Clip Gallery window appears **(14.3)**. It automatically opens to the My Pictures directory and displays the image files in that directory.

3. At the bottom of the Clip Gallery, select one of the three available options **(14.4)**. The Copy option places a copy of the image file into the Clip Gallery. Move Into actually moves the file into the Clip Gallery folder. Let Clip Gallery Find This Clip in Its Current Folder or Volume leaves the file in its current location.

(T) I P   *continues*

When selecting the images for import, hold down the Control key to select multiple images—it will save you a great deal of time and clicking!

Adding Images to the Clip Gallery continued

4. Click the Import button, and the Clip Properties window for the first image file selected opens, displaying a short description including the file type and size. A preview image of the file might appear in the box to the right (14.5).

5. Type a short description of the file in the Description box (14.6). Use the keywords you might use to find an image of this type in the future—without keywords, the images won't be found in a search.

6. Click on the Categories tab to assign the image to a pre-existing category (14.7).

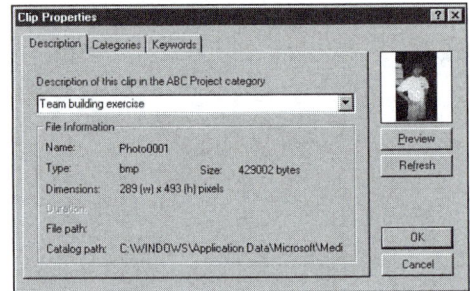

14.5

Some file formats will not show up as thumbnails because PhotoDraw can't peek inside to show you a preview. So, don't worry if you don't see a thumbnail of the image. The image is there and you can go ahead and import it.

Click here if you are importing more than one file and want the attributes on each of the files to be identical.

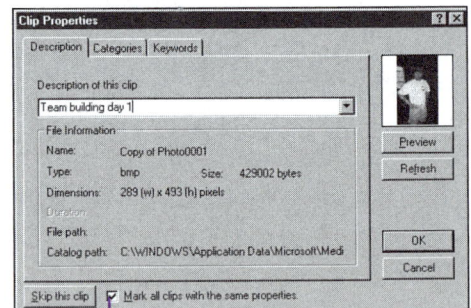

14.6

(T) I P

Be careful about using the Move Into option because when you delete a file that was moved into the Clip Gallery, PhotoDraw deletes the preview as well as the file itself. Unless you're critically short on hard drive space, leave it on the default Copy into Clip Gallery—this is the best option.

You can place a preview of a file in more than one category by clicking on multiple categories in the list. Multiple categories are useful if the image fits into several themes and you prefer using categories to searching with keywords.

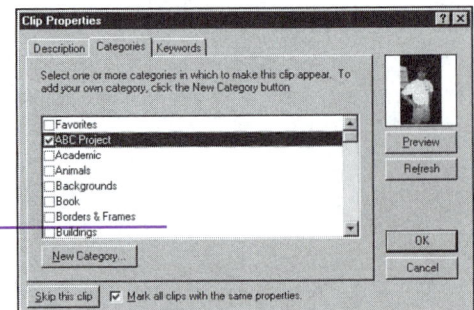

14.7

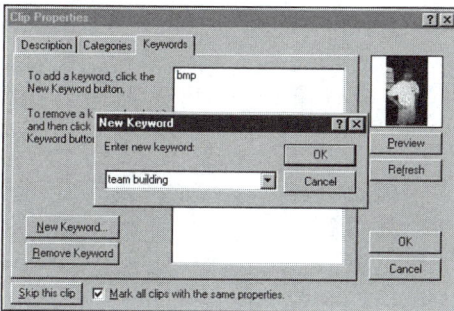

14.8

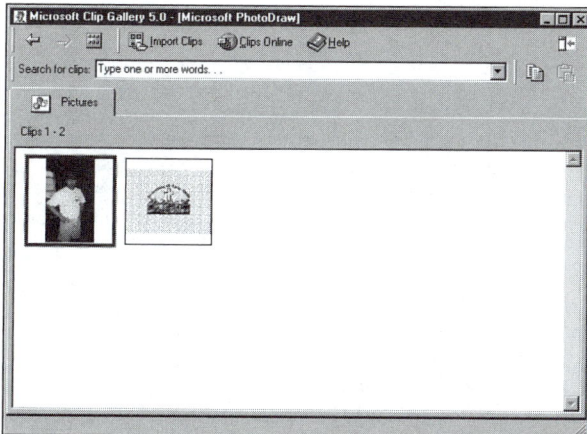

14.9   **To remove a preview image from the Clip Gallery, right-click the preview and select Delete from the pop-up menu.**

7. Click on the Keywords tab to create or assign an existing keyword to the file (14.8).

8. When you have finished assigning attributes to each file, previews of the imported files will appear in the Clip Gallery window (14.9).

(N) O T E

If you have selected more than one file to add to the Clip Gallery, PhotoDraw will ask you to repeat steps 4 through 6 for each image.

Changing or Deleting a Category

If you reorganize your clips, you might want to change or rename a category in the Clip Gallery to reflect the new organizational scheme. That's where the value of knowing how to change a category comes in. In addition, when you finish a project or move images off your hard disk into an archive somewhere else, you will want to do some housekeeping and remove a category of images.

1. Open the Clip Gallery and right-click on the category you want to change the name of. Select Rename Category from the pop-up menu.

2. Type the new name of the category in the Rename Category dialog box that appears (14.10), and then click OK. The icon appears in the Clip Gallery with the new name under it.

3. To delete the icon for a category of images, right-click on the category you want to remove, and select Delete Category (14.11).

4. PhotoDraw displays a message that says the icon will be deleted but not the files in the category. Click OK to finish the task or Cancel to abort the procedure.

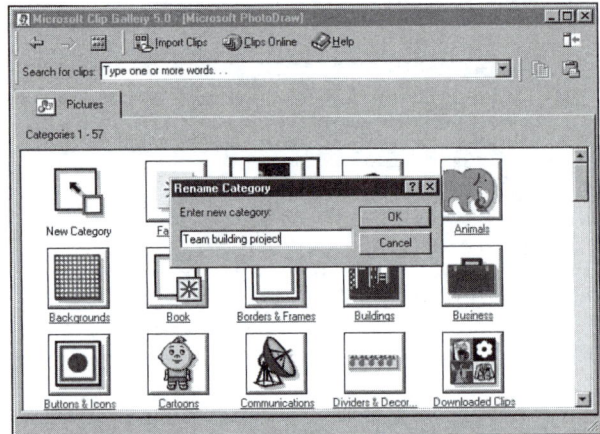

14.10

Pay extra attention here, especially if you didn't create the category you're deleting. If the Move Into option was used when the image was moved into the category, the image file is deleted along with the category, and PhotoDraw will not warn you it's about to delete the file itself.

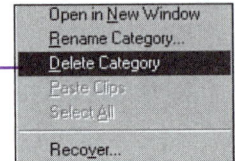

14.11

Restoring Deleted Categories or Image Clips

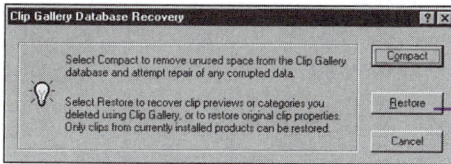

14.12 When you restore a clip, you're restoring the file pointer that PhotoDraw has been keeping that tells it where to find your file. The image file itself must be in the same place on the hard disk it was when you first created the pointer—otherwise, PhotoDraw won't find the image file.

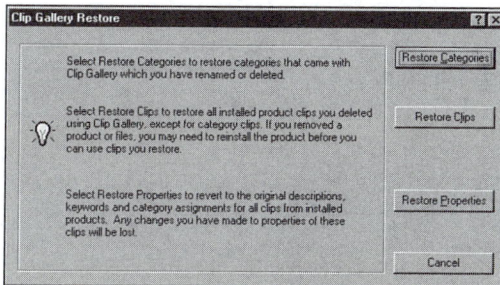

14.13 To recover files from an application or folder you have deleted from your computer, you must first reinstall the application or copy the folder back onto your computer.

In your zeal to recover hard drive space or organize your graphics, you can accidentally delete a clip art category. PhotoDraw can restore the default clip art categories from your original CD-ROM, giving you back the original images and categories. It's important to note that this works only for the original categories and clip art—if you delete a custom category containing your work, it cannot be recovered. This is yet another reason to use the Copy function instead of Move when importing your graphics.

1. To restore clip previews or categories, open the Clip Gallery and right-click any category icon. Select Recover from the pop-up menu. Click on the Restore button on the Clip Gallery Database Recovery window (14.12).

2. To restore deleted category icons, click on the Restore Categories button (14.13). To restore deleted image files, click on the Restore Clips button. Click on OK to accept the changes.

3. To restore the Clip Gallery to its original state (that is, to include all the categories that came in the software, but not the ones you've created), click on the Restore button on the Clip Gallery Database Recovery window.

Opening Multiple Categories

You might want to open more than one category at a time if you want to look at different images before you import them into a design. Or, you might want to compare stock images in one category to those in another to see whether you'd find another organizational scheme easier to use. You also can use this capability if you're creating identical sets of images for people to have access to for projects and want to be sure that the categories are identical; opening multiple file windows allows you to quickly double-check to be sure that you've done your filing properly.

14.14

1. Open the Clip Gallery, right-click on one of the icons of the categories you want to open, and select Open in a New Window from the pop-up menu. A new window with the previews of the images in that category appears (14.14).

2. Return to the Clip Gallery All Categories window by clicking somewhere in that window, and repeat the procedure to open a window for each of the categories needed (14.15).

3. To avoid cluttering your screen with too many windows, open only a few categories at a time, and size the windows so that you can see at least a few of the icons in each category.

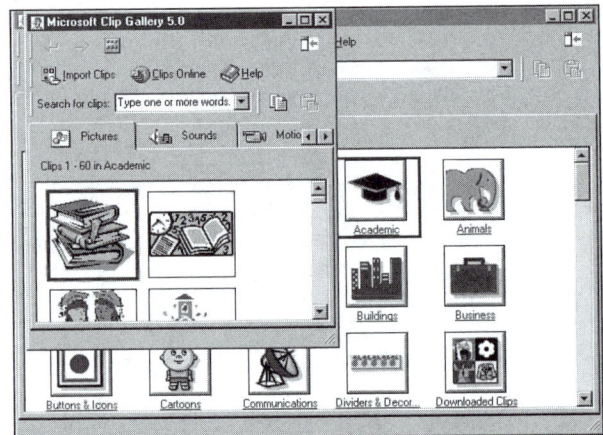

14.15

Using Keywords to Search for Images

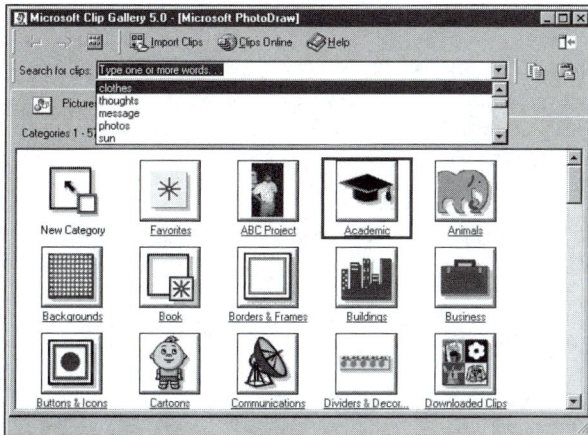

14.16

Like any image database, the Clip Gallery gives you the option of searching for images by using a keyword—a word that describes the image you're looking for in general terms. For example, the keyword *tools* might turn up images of men working, a hammer, a saw, or even a pocketknife.

The images already in the Clip Gallery have been assigned keywords, and you should add keywords (a procedure described later) to each new image you add to the Gallery.

1. Open the Clip Gallery (Insert→Clip Art) and click the down-arrow key next to Search for Clips to access the list of keywords most recently used for searches in this Clip Gallery (14.16).

2. Scroll through the list of words until you find one that describes, in general, the image you'd like to find. When you find it, click on the word to start a search for images with that keyword.

3. If you can't find a keyword that describes the image you're looking for, type your word in the box and press Enter to start the search.

continues

Using Keywords to Search for Images continued

4. If PhotoDraw finds any images associated with that keyword, it displays the search results in the Clip Gallery window **(14.17)**.

5. Scroll through the display of images and click on one to select it for use in your design. When you click on it, a small icon menu appears. Click on the first icon to put the image into your design **(14.18)**.

PhotoDraw displays the number of images found that match the keyword in the upper-left side of the window.

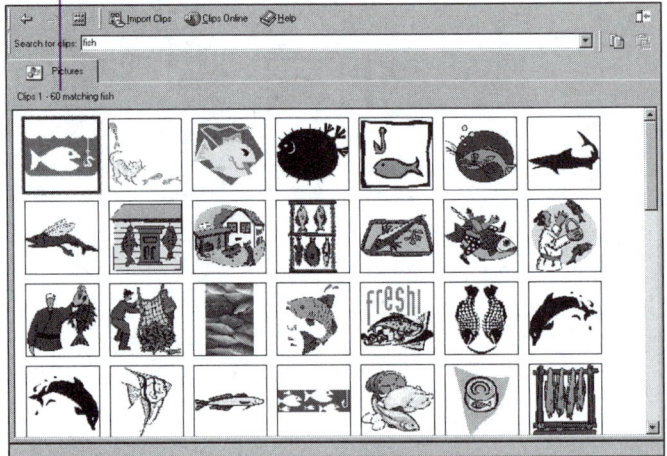

14.17

Click on the first icon to insert the image into your design. Click on the second to get an enlarged preview of the image. Click on the third one to put the image into another category, or click on the fourth one to find images that are similar in artistic style to this one but that have other keywords associated with them.

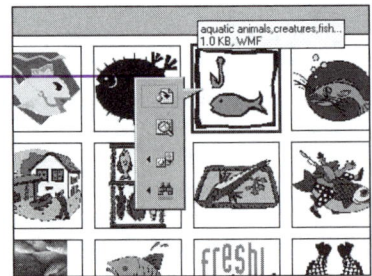

14.18

(N) O T E

If PhotoDraw does not find any images with that keyword, it displays a message to that effect, and you can search again using a different word.

Adding Keywords for Searching

14.19

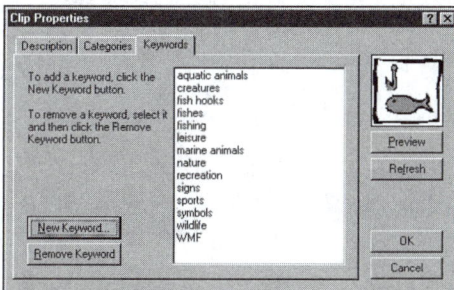

14.20

Ⓝ O T E

To add a keyword to an image as you are adding the image to the Clip Gallery, click on the Import Clips button on the Clip Gallery window and follow steps 3 and 4.

You might want to develop your own set of keywords to add to images in the Clip Gallery that already have other keywords associated with them. Although the keywords in the Clip Gallery are good ones, by adding your own, you can use keywords that make sense to you or are relevant to a particular project. For example, if you want to remember all images you used for a certain project, you would use the name of the project as a keyword for each of those images.

1. Open the Clip Gallery (Insert→Clip Art) and locate the image to which you want to add a keyword.

2. Right-click on the image and a pop-up menu of options appears (14.19). Select Clip Properties from the bottom of the list.

3. The Clip Properties window opens. Click on the Keywords tab to open the keyword information (14.20). The list of keywords already associated with that image is shown.

4. Click on the New Keyword button and the New Keyword window opens. Type the keyword you want to use and click OK. PhotoDraw adds that word to the list. Click OK to end the process.

©HAPTER 15

In this chapter you will learn how to...

Change Print Sizes and Positions

Print a Single Image

Change the Print Quality

Print a Picture to a File

Print the Same Image Multiple Times or Multiple Images on a Single Sheet

With the prices of color printers constantly falling, it seems everyone has one—which is fantastic, because color enhances any document. Information presented in color is 30% more likely to be remembered, making it a critical element in your business presentations. With the quality of photo output nearly matching that of a photo lab, memories are even easier to capture, collect, and present in a variety of ways.

PRINTING YOUR IMAGES

You have several ways to print images after you are finished creating them. The options run from the standard of printing what you see onscreen to printing the image to a file, all the way through to printing multiple copies of a single image (or multiple copies of multiple images) on a single sheet.

Some of the printing options are so simple and so similar to printing options in other Microsoft programs that no specific directions are necessary. The functions covered in this chapter are the ones that are not so obvious or simple.

In this chapter, you will learn how to change the print size and position of an image and how to make a single image from a page of images print on a sheet by itself. You will also learn how to add crop marks to images, change the overall print quality, print to a file so that the image file can be printed by a printing company, and fill a sheet with multiple copies of one or more images.

Changing Print Sizes and Positions

You have to specify a background size when you create a new file in PhotoDraw, and most of the time you'll opt for letter-size because that's probably the size of paper you're using. You can change the page size after you have created the image, however, and you have a few other ways to control how the image prints.

1. Open the PhotoDraw file that contains the image you want to print. Choose File→Print and then select the Size tab on the Print window (15.1).

2. If you want PhotoDraw to scale the image so that it fits the entire page, select the Fit to Page option (15.2).

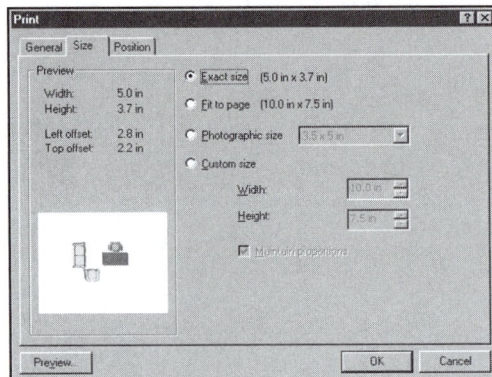

15.1

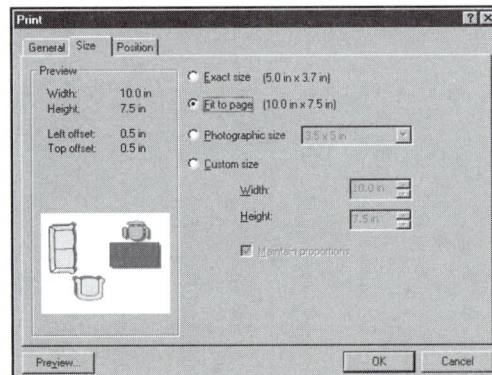

15.2　If you want the new image size to have the same overall proportions as the original, type only one dimension and click the Maintain Proportions check box off and back on. PhotoDraw calculates the other dimension for you.

T I P

If your image is small yet extremely detailed (high DPI) and you want the details to be obvious, enlarging the image to fit the page size can help. This will require at least one test print—extreme enlargement can drop overall image quality, so always test first before making your final print.

N O T E

Making changes to the print size of a file does not change the size of the image itself or make permanent changes to the file.

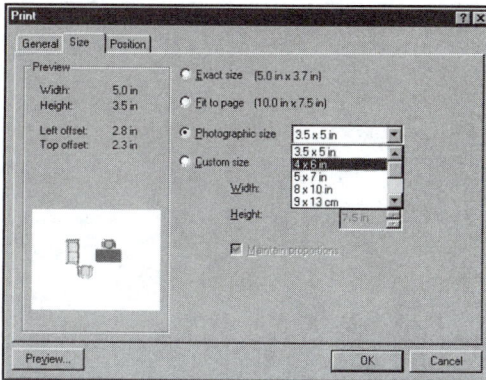

15.3

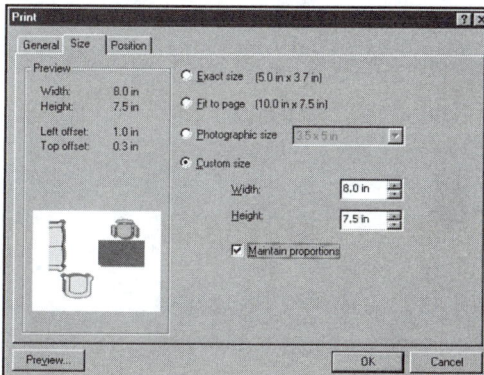

15.4

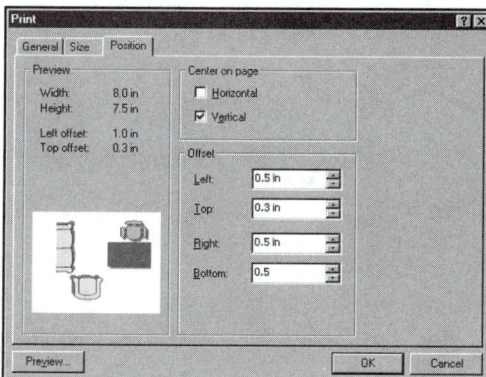

15.5

3. If you want PhotoDraw to scale the image so that it is the size of a standard photographic image (such as 4 inches by 6 inches), select the Photographic Size option and then select the size you want from the pull-down menu **(15.3)**.

4. If you want a completely different print size for the image, click on Custom Size and manually enter the Height and Width dimensions you want the image enlarged or reduced to **(15.4)**.

5. To change where on the page the image is printed, click on the Position tab and enter the coordinates where you want the image to be placed on the page **(15.5)**. Use this option when you want to control where the image is printed— say, to avoid running into a logo on letterhead.

6. When you've finished making your selections and changes, click OK. PhotoDraw sends the print file to the printer and the image prints.

PhotoDraw gives you a small-scale preview of the effect of the changes when you change position coordinates. To see a full-screen preview of the effects of the changes, click on the Preview button.

Printing a Single Image

You can easily select a single image from a page with multiple images and print the image on a page by itself if the image you want to print does not overlap any of the other images on the page.

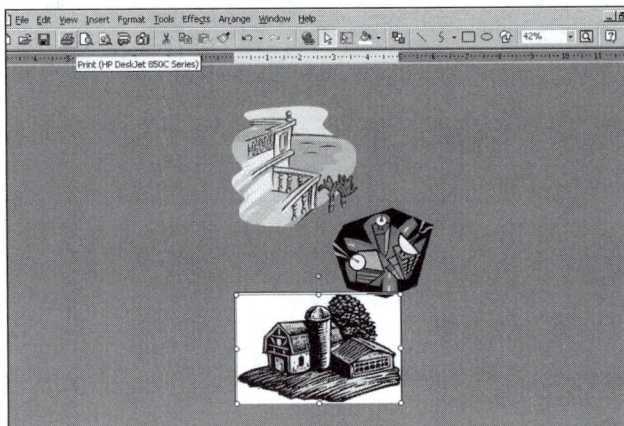

15.6

1. Click on the object you want to print. Select View→Fit Picture Area to Selection. The image you want to print is selected, and a white rectangle fills the space behind the image (15.6).

2. Click the Print icon on the main toolbar to print the image. Choose File→Print if you need to make size or position changes as outlined in the previous task.

3. To restore the original background area, select Edit→Undo after you've printed the image.

(T) I P

If you are printing one image on a page, you might want to add crop marks to the image so that you can trim away the excess paper neatly. To add crop marks around the image, select Print Crop Marks on the General tab that appears when you select File→Print.

Changing the Print Quality

If you don't see the resolution you want to use, click on the Properties button to access your printer control software and to set the desired resolution.

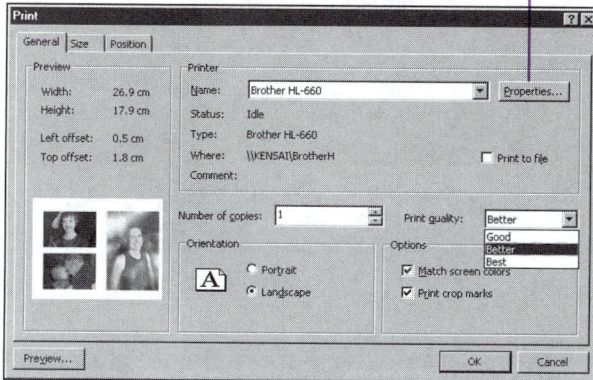

15.7

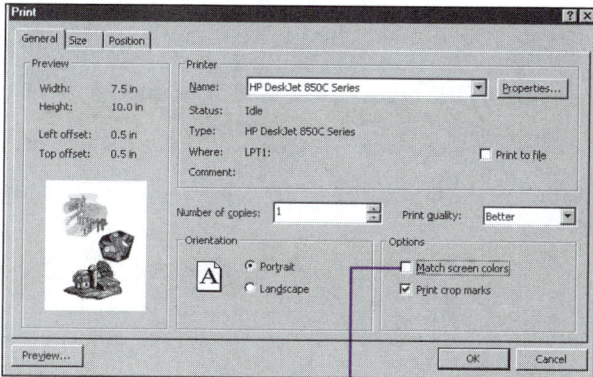

15.8

Leave Color Matching on unless you've been given a good reason to turn it off. If your computer monitor and printer are using the Image Color Matching (ICM) available under Windows 95, when Color Matching is active, PhotoDraw uses the correct device profiles. If the ICM profiles are not present, Color Matching doesn't work whether it's selected or not.

PhotoDraw gives you two ways to affect the overall appearance of a print job: changing the resolution/ print quality and turning color matching on and off. Use these controls to get the most out of your printer, including the highest possible resolution and control over the final appearance.

For example, if you are printing a draft copy of an image, you might want to print at 100dpi to save toner or ink. On the other hand, if you have a digital photo image that is 600dpi and want to see all of that quality in the printout, you'll need to be sure that the print resolution is set to 600dpi.

1. To change the print resolution of an image, select one of the three options in the Print Quality drop-down list found on the General tab of the Print dialog box.

2. Select (Good) to print at draft quality and (Best) to print at maximum print quality; (Better) is the default (15.7).

3. To turn color matching off, deselect the Match Screen Colors box (15.8). By default, PhotoDraw keeps Color Matching active.

Printing a Picture to a File

PhotoDraw can save an image file as a printer file (PRN) that you can send to someone so that they can print your file without needing PhotoDraw.

1. On the General tab of the Print dialog box, select the Print to File check box and click OK (15.9). The Print to File Dialog box opens.

2. Select the location for PhotoDraw to save the printer file to (15.10).

3. Type a name for the print file in the File Name box (15.11), and click Save to start the process.

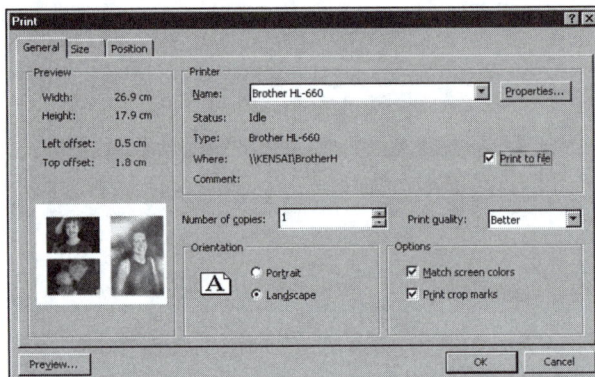

15.9

15.10

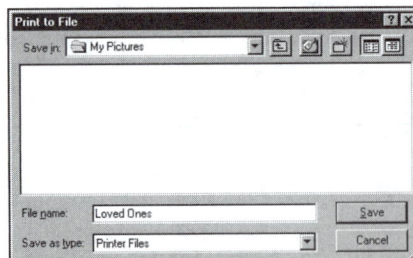

15.11

(T) I P

Select all other print options before you print a file to disk, such as print quality, because PhotoDraw will record these settings in the PRN file.

(N) O T E

You can't open or view a PRN file, so don't use this file format if you want to perform these functions later. Save the file in native PhotoDraw format for later use in PhotoDraw, or in EPS if you want to be able to view the file in another program.

Using the Reprint Option

15.12

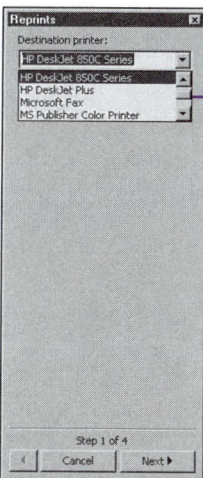

It is important to know what kind of printer the file will be printed to in order to select that printer in the menu because the file will contain print information specific to that printer.

15.13

PhotoDraw can copy your image file and print smaller versions of the file on a single sheet of paper, or other media such as labels, CD stickers, and so on. The name of this function is a little misleading, because it's used for a lot more than reprinting—if you need to print address labels for example, this is the only place to do it.

1. Choose File→Print Reprints. PhotoDraw launches a procedure wizard to help you complete the process **(15.12)**.

2. Select a printer for the print job from the drop-down menu, and click Next to continue to the next step **(15.13)**.

continues

(T) I P

At the end of this procedure, PhotoDraw automatically prints your sheet, so have the sheet of paper in your printer before you begin.

(T) I P

Use this feature to create labels, business cards, and other projects in which you want to fill an entire sheet with the same image, or want to fit it to a custom or preprinted sheet.

Using the Reprint Option continued

3. Select the template you want to use for printing the job. Select a template and page orientation and click Next (15.14).

4. Tell PhotoDraw whether you want to use one image to fill the page or whether you want to use more than one image on the same page. Select One or Many and click Next to proceed (15.15). PhotoDraw fills a page with multiple solid rectangles to hold the images. A Picture List of recently used images appears on the left side of the screen.

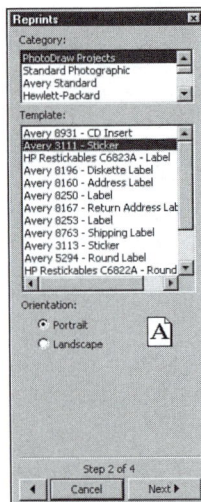

15.14

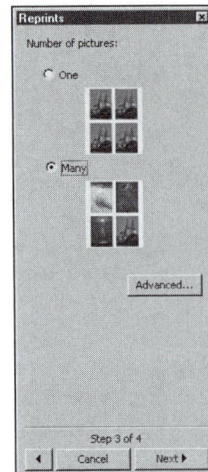

15.15

5. If you want the image to fit within the rectangle area, click on the Fit Within option (15.16). This will force the image to be scaled down with its dimensions constrained—it won't look "stretched."

6. If you want the image to completely fill the rectangle area, click on the Fill option (15.17). Unless your image is equal to or smaller than the print size, some cropping will occur.

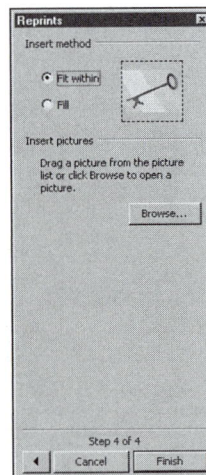

15.16

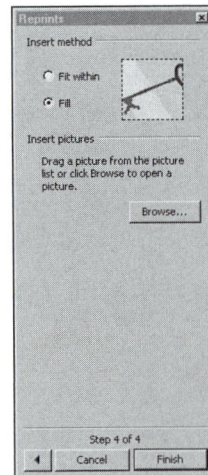

15.17

(N) O T E

Click the Advanced button if you want to change the spacing between the images.

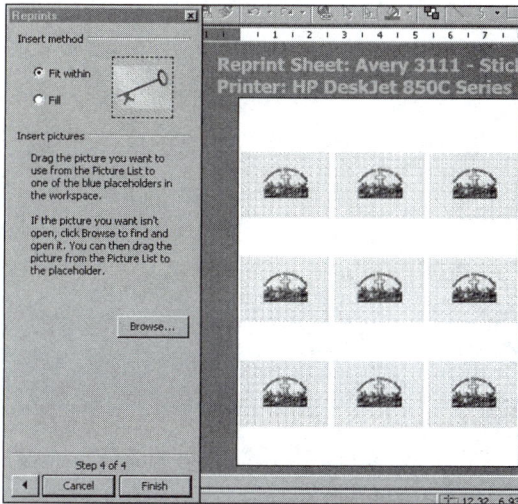

15.18

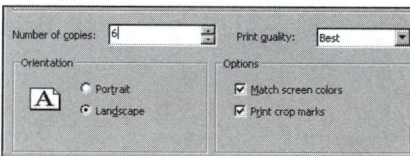

15.19

7. Select your image (or images) from the picture list, or browse the Clip Gallery or hard disk. If you selected One on the earlier step, PhotoDraw fills the sheet with copies of the image **(15.18)**. If you selected Many, you must fill each rectangle one at a time.

8. Click Finish to complete the procedure. PhotoDraw prints your sheet immediately.

(T) I P

To print more than one copy of a single image or page, increase the number of copies on the Print window **(15.19)**.

(N) O T E

PhotoDraw comes with many templates for Avery and Hewlett-Packard label stocks and other specialty items such as business cards.

©HAPTER 16

When version 1.0 of PhotoDraw came out, it offered a full set of tools for creating and editing images. These tools included drawing and painting tools for all kinds of pictures and the capability to quickly and painlessly correct image problems. PhotoDraw 1.0 also included many ways to create and edit images bound for Web pages and Web sites.

NEW WEB GRAPHICS FEATURES IN VERSION 2.0

In version 2.0, Microsoft added new capabilities to the program, including new editing tools and new ways to alter designs. Specifically in the Web area, the new tools for Web effects allow for impressive effects—highlight, glow, emboss, and styles all allow for unique customization of your images.

Other new Web features include JavaScript rollover effects—if you've ever moved your mouse cursor over an image and watched it change or move, you've seen a rollover effect. Animated GIFs are like little movies, playing frame by frame, that you can create with PhotoDraw. Although challenging to create, they are highly effective at communicating information online.

You will also learn how to create image maps by adding a hyperlink to an image, enabling you to create navigation maps that allow visitors to click on different parts of a photo of image to navigate around your site. Last, you'll learn how to edit and delete hyperlinks.

Wherever possible, these new features are discussed in other chapters of this book. This chapter covers the version 2.0–only features related to Web graphics.

Creating an Animated GIF

An animated GIF is, quite simply, a series of individual GIF files strung together into a single file, much like an old 8mm motion picture is a series of still images. Each animated GIF frame is an individual image, so when it goes through the frames, it's like watching a movie—the closer it gets to 30 frames per second (FPS), the more it looks like a movie clip. The human eye starts to notice visual problems with motion around 26 FPS. If you've visited just about any site on the Web, you've probably encountered an animated GIF. Most of the time, it is an image or text that moves by itself and stays in motion the entire time you're looking at the Web page, although some will be in motion for a given number of cycles before going still. Animated GIFs, used carefully, are a good way to attract attention to a particular area of a Web page.

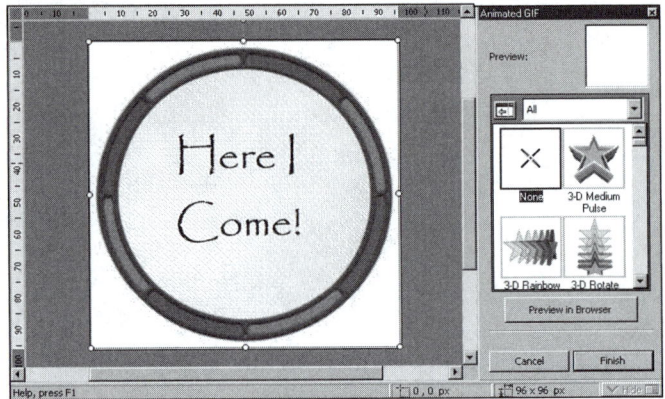

16.1

It's critical to keep the images fast loading and carefully planned out—there's nothing more visually confusing than seeing multiple animated GIFs on the same page, moving in different patterns and timings. It's the equivalent of virtual seasickness.

1. Open the file containing the image you want to animate, and click on the image to select it. Select Effects→Animated GIF and the Animated GIF workpane opens (16.1).

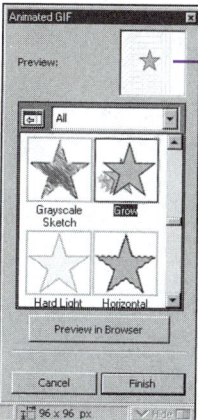

A sample of the effect in action is seen in the preview window in the top of the workpane.

16.2

2. Scroll through the possible effects and select the one you want to use by clicking on it (16.2).

3. Click the Finish button when you have made your selection. PhotoDraw starts the Save Animated GIF Wizard. (16.3).

4. Click the Next button to proceed to the next step in the wizard. In nearly every case, choose Optimized Palette (16.4).

continues

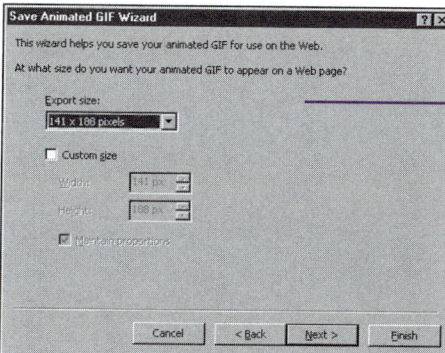

16.3

Click the down-arrow button in the window to see the various image sizes available to you.

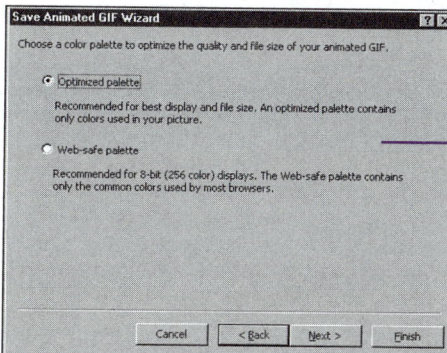

16.4

Most computers are in 16-bit or higher color modes, so the Web-Safe Palette will only drag down the overall quality of your image.

(T) I P

Unless you need to have the animated GIF be larger than the original image, leave the size at its default setting. This size is large enough to attract attention without being overwhelming, but experiment with different sizes if you feel the default size is too small. Keep in mind that file size is the biggest constraint with animated GIFs. People won't wait two minutes just to see one image! If an animated GIF goes over 50KB in file size, you're going to lose much of your audience.

Creating an Animated GIF continued

5. Click the Next button to continue. PhotoDraw attempts to decide for you whether the image should be transparent or not. If you'd like your image to "float" on the Web page with the background visible behind it, choose the first option, and follow through to the next step and choose the background color of your site (16.5).

6. Click the Next button and alter the animation settings of the image, if desired, by adjusting the controls (16.6).

7. Click the Next button or the Finish button to finish saving your animated GIF file.

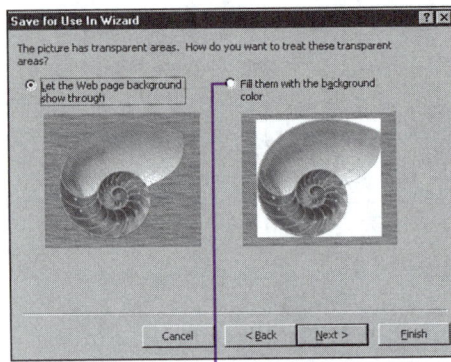

16.5 You can force the areas that would normally be transparent to be colored by selecting this option, clicking Next, and choosing a color to fill the transparent areas.

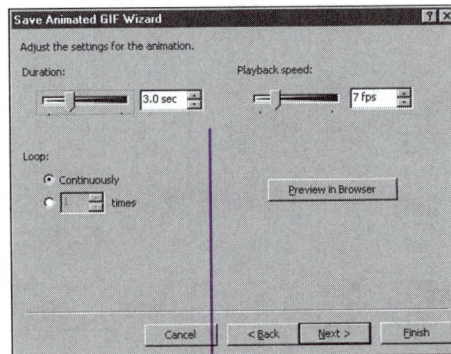

16.6

The options here will have a great impact on your final file size. If you choose a high frame rate, your overall image will greatly go up in size. Alternatively, you can choose a longer or shorter duration—this will also affect file size. It's simple math—a five-second clip at 25 FPS will have 125 GIF files in it, making it a very large image. As a rule of thumb, clips with a short duration but fairly high frame rate (10-18 FPS) will look the best, but experiment a few times before making your decision.

(T) I P

Animated GIFs shouldn't continue the same action for too long a period—usually three to five loops is enough, unless the image is on the splash page of a Web site, in which case endless looping is more appropriate. As a rule of thumb, always test your animations by having friends and family look at them before showing them to others.

Creating a Rollover Button

16.7 **When you apply the effect, you will see only the first stage of the effect on your object unless you click the Preview in Browser button on the Rollover workpane.**

In version 1.0, you could create buttons for Web pages, but you could not add a nice feature called rollover to the buttons. PhotoDraw 2.0 lets you create buttons with rollover capabilities. Rollover buttons are the ones you see on Web pages that change appearance when you move over or click on them. Using rollover buttons on your Web page instead of static ones is a good way to add visual interest.

1. First, open the file that has the image you want to add the rollover effect to, and click on the image. Then, select Effects→Rollover and the Rollover workpane appears.

2. Scroll through the gallery of rollover effects. Click on one to open a preview window in the workpane and see a preview of the appearance change. Double-click on a thumbnail of the effect to apply it to your object **(16.7)**.

continues

(N) O T E

Unless you first click on the image you want to apply the effect to, the Effects menu is grayed out and you won't be able to select anything on the menu.

Creating a Rollover Button continued

3. After you've applied an effect, save the file by choosing File→Save for Use In and then selecting On the Web, and then As a Web Page from the list of options that appear **(16.8)**.

4. For things such as buttons and art that use fewer than 256 colors, choose GIF on the Save for Use In wizard. For photographic images that use thousands of colors, choose a high-quality JPEG setting **(16.9)**.

5. The final step in the wizard confirms all your settings, and clicking Save brings up the filenaming dialog box. Type a filename, click Save, and it will render all three of your images and generate an HTML page for you with the proper code to insert into your Web site to enable the rollover to work properly.

(T) I P

PhotoDraw doesn't do a very good job of optimizing the GIF images—if you're serious about creating GIF animations such as banner ads for Web sites, look at GIF ANIMATOR by Ulead. It enables you to optimize the image, resulting in 30%-70% smaller files, control how long each frame is displayed, and offers many other powerful options. You can download a 30-day demo from `http://www.ulead.com/ga`.

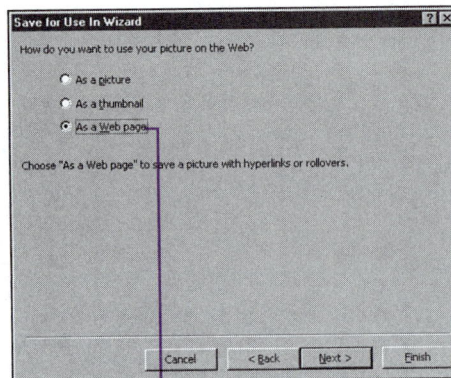

16.8 **When you select As a Web Page, PhotoDraw tells you it will save the image with the rollover attached.**

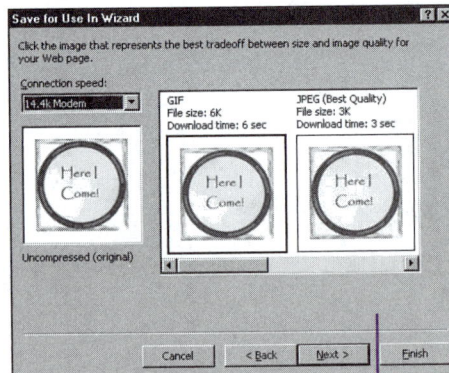

16.9 **The Save for Use In wizard gives you the choice of file type and size when saving your files for the Web.**

Creating an Imagemap

16.10

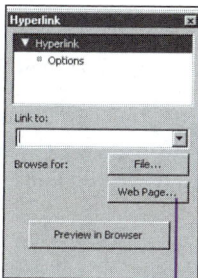

16.11

You can click on the Web Page button on the Hyperlink workpane to launch your browser and find your way to the Web page to which you want to establish a link. After you've seen the page in the browser, Alt+Tab back to PhotoDraw, and it automatically enters the correct linking information.

Sometimes, instead of using buttons or underlined links on a Web page to link to other sites or pages within your site, you might want to use an imagemap. An imagemap is generally a large image made up of a group of smaller objects. When someone clicks on part of the image (commonly called a "hotspot"), the browser moves to the linked page or site for that area. You can even apply a rollover effect to a hotspot if you want the image to change appearance when someone clicks or hovers over it.

1. Open the file containing the images you want to add an imagemap to, and press Ctrl+A to select all elements. It's important that the image you're using has multiple parts to it—you can't make an imagemap out of a single, large image. You should see multiple selection boxes after you press Ctrl+A (16.10).

2. Select Insert→Hyperlink to open the Hyperlink workpane (16.11). If this choice is grayed out, it means you haven't selected your image properly.

continues

Creating an Imagemap continued

3. Click on the object you want to be a hotspot, and then enter the URL of the Web site (be sure to include the `http://`) or the location and name of the file you want to link to (such as `C:\Webfiles\aboutme.htm`) in the Link To box on the workpane.

4. Click on the Options selection on the workpane to put in the text that will appear in the status bar at the bottom of the browser when the user moves the mouse over the object, and the Alternative (alt) text **(16.12)** that appears in a pop-up box when the user hovers over the image.

5. After you've finished assigning hotspots to the various parts of the image, go to File→Save For Use In, and then select On the Web, and finally, As a Web Page. You have the choice of transparency—pick the appropriate option for your graphic. Click Save on the last step of the wizard, and PhotoDraw will generate an HTML file and all the graphic files you need for your imagemap.

Alternative text is also important for visually impaired users—their special Web browsers read the alt text aloud so they can "see" what the image is. It also improves your ranking in some search engines, so describe the image carefully!

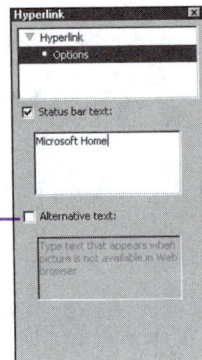

16.12

(N) O T E

Add a rollover effect to the image to which you have added an imagemap if you want the image to change appearance when someone clicks on it.

Editing and Deleting a Hyperlink

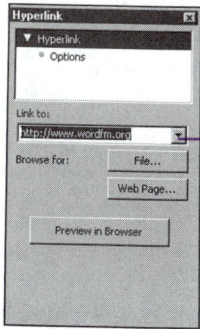

The existing linking information is displayed on the workpane.

16.13

Nothing stays the same, and because the Web changes faster than almost anything else, you'll need to make some changes to your hyperlinks from time to time to keep up with site address changes. Although doing this in your HTML editor is likely the best way after all the graphics are finished, you can use PhotoDraw 2000 to regenerate the imagemap code and graphics.

1. Open the file containing the hyperlinked image, and click on the part of the image that has the hyperlink you need to change.

2. Select Insert→Hyperlink to open the Hyperlink workpane (16.13).

3. Change or delete the linking information as desired.

4. Close the workpane. Choose File→Save for Use In and select As a Web Page to save the image and preserve the hyperlink.

(T) I P

Don't forget to update or change the associated text information as needed by clicking on Options on the Hyperlink workpane when you update or change the link itself.

INDEX

SYMBOLS

3D command (Effects menu), 146

3D objects
converting from 2D objects, 146
edges, thicknesses, 148-149
fills, applying, 150
lighting effects, 152
rotation of, 151
text, applying, 147-148, 153
tilt of, 151

3D workpane, 146-147
edge effects, 148-149
fill effects, 150
lighting effects, 152
rotate and tilt effects, 151
text effects, 148, 153

A

adding
arrows to lines, 113
colors
custom color palettes, 169-171
to shadows, 159
fill effects in geometric shapes, 114-115
images (Clip Gallery), 199-201
keywords (Clip Gallery), 207
shadows to objects, 156
shapes to images, 116

Align command (Arrange menu), 20, 37

aligning
objects, 20-21
text (Text workpane), 30
text objects, 37

alternate text on Web pages, image replacement, 226

animated GIFs
creating, 220-222
frames per second (FPS), 220-222
loop frequency, 222
size constraints, 221
Ulead GIF ANIMATOR, 224

antique photographic effects, 123-124

applying
3D effects to text objects, 147-148, 153
Designer Effects
single, 120
to images, 122
edges
to clip art, 143
to objects (Edge workpane), 136-137
effects to partial images, 121
fills
to 3D objects, 150
to clip art, 143
painting effects to clip art, 100-101
shapes to images, 116
special effects to photographs (Designer Effects workpane), 73-74
text objects
artistic fills (Artistic Fill workpane), 51